HOMOS

HOMOS

◆

Leo Bersani

Harvard University Press

Cambridge, Massachusetts

London, England

1995

Designed by Marianne Perlak in Sabon and Weiss

This book is printed on acid-free paper, and its binding
materials have been chosen for strength and durability.

Library of Congress Cataloging-in-Publication Data

Bersani, Leo.

Homos/Leo Bersani.

p. cm.

Includes bibliographical references and index.

ISBN 0-674-40619-2 (alk. paper)

1. Homosexuality—Philosophy. 2. Gay men—Psychology.
3. Homosexuality in literature. I. Title.

HQ76.B52 1995

305.9′06642—dc20

94-30987

CIP

For Sam Geraci

Contents

DR DIXON *(Reads a bill of health.)* Professor Bloom is a finished example of the new womanly man. . . . He is about to have a baby. . . .

BLOOM O, I so want to be a mother.

MRS THORNTON *(In nursetender's gown.)* Embrace me tight, dear. You'll be soon over it. Tight, dear. *(Bloom embraces her tightly and bears eight male yellow and white children. They appear on a redcarpeted staircase adorned with expensive plants. All are handsome, with valuable metallic faces, wellmade, respectably dressed and wellconducted, speaking five modern languages fluently and interested in various arts and sciences.)*

—James Joyce, *Ulysses*

Familles, je vous hais!

—André Gide, *Les Nourritures terrestres*

Prologue: "We"

No one wants to be called a homosexual. The revulsion that designation would inspire in a Christian fundamentalist is understandable. Given the pressures and privileges intrinsic to the position one occupies on the great homo-heterosexual divide in our society, we can also appreciate the anxiety, on the part of those straights most openly sympathetic with gay causes, not to be themselves mistaken for one of those whose rights they commendably defend. It is even possible to sympathize with all the closeted gay men and lesbians who fear, rightly or wrongly, personal and professional catastrophe were they to be exposed as homosexuals. Much more mystifying is the aversion to "homosexuality" on the part of self-identified homosexual activists and theorists. Not only that: those I have in mind, far from proposing merely lexical substitutions (gay or queer, say, instead of homosexual), are also insisting that their chosen self-designations no longer designate the reality we might assume to be indissolubly connected to whatever term is used. For the interested but theoretically uninitiated observer of today's cultural scene, it may come as something of an epistemological shock to learn, from Monique Wittig, that "it would be incorrect to say that lesbians associate, make love, live with women"; or, from Judith Butler, that the only thing lesbians have in common is a knowledge of how homophobia works against women; or, from Michael Warner, that queerness is characterized by a determined "resistance to regimes of the normal."[1] These assertions, made by three of the most original writers working today on questions of sexuality and gender, suggest a definitional crisis. Is the "homophobic lesbian" an oxymoron? And since we have all known men who lust for other men while otherwise feeling quite comfortable with "regimes of the normal," is *queer* now to be taken as delineating political rather than erotic tendencies? No longer would a boy discover that, whether he likes it or not, he is queer; indeed, all of us—even after decades of what we thought of as extravagant sexual confirmation of our queerness—would have to earn the right to that designation and to the dignity it now confers.

In much of this book I will be arguing that these reformulations should be both welcomed and resisted. Although it would be easy to discuss them as evidence of a paranoid distrust of all self-identifying moves, there are excellent historical reasons for such distrust. The elaborating of certain erotic preferences into a "character"—into a kind of erotically determined essence—can never be a disinterested scientific enterprise. The attempted stabilizing of identity is inherently a disciplinary project. Panoptic vision depends on a successful immobilizing of the human objects it surveys, and, in an argument made familiar by Michel Foucault, sexuality now provides the principal categories for a strategic transformation of behavior into manipulatable characterological types. Once "the homosexual" *and* "the heterosexual" were seen as primary examples of such types, it was perhaps inevitable that any effort to enclose human subjects within clearly delimited and coherent identities would become suspect.

While conceived as an act of resistance to homophobic oppression, the project of elaborating a gay identity could itself be discredited. For hasn't that identity been exclusionary, delineating what is easily recognizable as a white, middle-class, liberal gay identity? And wasn't the delineating act itself a sign, or rather an intellectual symptom, of the very class it described? Merely looking for a gay identity predetermined the field in which it would be found, since the leisured activity of looking characterized the identity it sought to uncover. "Gay identity" led many of those invited to recognize themselves as belonging to it (as well as those excluded) to protest that there are many ways of being gay, that sexual behavior is never only a question of sex, that it is embedded in all the other, nonsexual ways in which we are socially and culturally positioned. An intentionally oppositional gay identity, by its very coherence, only repeats the restrictive and immobilizing analyses it set out to resist.

Even more: why should sexual preference be the key to identity in the first place? And, more fundamentally, why should preference itself be understood only as a function of the homo-heterosexual dyad? That dyad imprisons the eroticized body within a rigidly gendered sexuality, in which pleasure is at once recognized and legitimized as a function of genital differences between the sexes. Finally, as Warner has noted, in such a system gender difference becomes "a sign of the irreducible phenomenological difference between persons."[2] The portentous consequences of buying into the "homosexual" designation should now be clear: that term is a central piece in the profoundly biased cultural education we receive in sameness and difference—that is, in our self-forming perceptions of where we end and others begin, and where and how the frictions of otherness block the expansion of our selves.

And yet, if these suspicions of identity are necessary, they are not necessarily liberating. Gay men and lesbians have nearly disappeared into their sophisticated awareness of how they have been *constructed as* gay men and lesbians. The discrediting of a specific gay identity (and the correlative distrust of etiological investigations into homosexuality) has had the curious but predictable result of eliminating the indispensable grounds for resistance to, precisely, hegemonic regimes of the normal. We have erased ourselves in the process of denaturalizing the epistemic and political regimes that have constructed us. The power of those systems is only minimally contested by demonstrations of their "merely" historical character. They don't need to be natural in order to rule; to demystify them doesn't render them inoperative. If many gays now reject a homosexual identity as it has been elaborated for gays by others, the dominant heterosexual society doesn't need our belief in its own naturalness in order to continue exercising and enjoying the privileges of dominance. Suspicious of our own enforced identity, we are reduced to playing subversively with normative identities—attempting, for example, to "resignify" the family for communities that defy the usual assumptions about what constitutes a family. These efforts, while valuable, can have assimilative rather than subversive consequences; having de-gayed themselves, gays melt into the culture they like to think of themselves as undermining. Or, having "realistically" abandoned what one queer theorist calls a "millennial vision" of domination's demise,[3] we resign ourselves to the micropolitics of local struggles for participatory democracy and social justice, thus revealing political ambitions about as stirring as those reflected on the bumper stickers that enjoin us to "think globally" and "act locally."

De-gaying gayness can only fortify homophobic oppression; it accomplishes in its own way the principal aim of homophobia: the elimination of gays. The consequence of self-erasure is . . . self-erasure. Even a provisional acceptance of the very categories elaborated by dominant identitarian regimes might more effectively undermine those forces than a simple disappearing act. For example, the category of homosexuality—even as it has been homophobically cultivated—includes within it an indeterminacy and a mobility inimical to the disciplinary designs facilitated by the assignment of stable identities. Furthermore, gay critiques of homosexual identity have generally been *desexualizing* discourses. You would never know, from most of the works I discuss, that gay men, for all their diversity, share a strong sexual interest in other human beings anatomically identifiable as male. Even recent attempts in queer theory to make sexuality "a primary category for social analysis"[4] has merely added another category to the analysis of social institutions (making explicit the prescriptive assumptions about sexuality embedded within institutions) rather than trying to trace the political productivity of the sexual. As I have written elsewhere, though it is indisputably true that sexuality is always being politicized, the ways in which *having sex* politicizes can be highly problematic.[5] How, for example, does a gay man's erotic joy in the penis inflect, or endanger, what he might like to think of as his insubordinate relation to the paternal phallus? In what ways does that joy both qualify and fortify his investment in the Law, in patriarchal structures of dominance and submission he might prefer to think of himself as only subverting?

It is perhaps unfortunate, but no less true, that we have *learned to desire* from within the heterosexual norms and gendered structures that we can no longer think of as natural, or as exhausting all the options for self-identification. Since deconstructing an imposed identity will not erase the habit of desire, it might be more profitable to test the resistance of the identity from *within* the desire. Although there are valid grounds for questioning the assumption that desire between men, or between women, is desire for "the same," it is also true that because our apprenticeship in desiring takes place within that assumption, homosexuality can become a privileged model of sameness—one that makes manifest not the limits but the inestimable value of relations of sameness, of homo-relations. Perhaps inherent in gay desire is a revolutionary inaptitude for heteroized sociality. This of course means sociality as we know it, and the most politically disruptive aspect of the homo-ness I will be exploring in gay desire is a redefinition of sociality so radical that it may appear to require a provisional withdrawal from relationality itself.

This difficult project will be ventured in Chapter 4 through works by Gide, Proust, and Genet, a discussion that should be thought of not as a more or less enjoyable addendum of literary criticism to the arguments made in the rest of this book but, instead, as absolutely crucial to the persuasiveness of those arguments. The writers I discuss are—in sharp contrast to contemporary gay and lesbian theorists—drawn to the *anticommunitarian* impulses they discover in homosexual desire. For them, otherness is articulated as relay stations in a process of self-extension. Far removed from our own theoretical debates, *The Immoralist, Sodome et Gomorrhe,* and *Funeral Rites* are nonetheless relevant to those debates in demonstrating how desire for the same can free us from an oppressive psychology of desire as lack (a psychology that grounds sociality in trauma and castration). New reflection on homo-ness could lead us to a salutary devalorizing of difference— or, more exactly, to a notion of difference not as a trauma to be overcome (a view that, among other things, nourishes antagonistic relations between the sexes), but rather as a nonthreatening supplement to sameness.

I discover, in rereading myself, that I have become an ambiguous "we"—a fact I both welcome and find somewhat troubling. Who are these others I repeatedly add to myself? If they share my own identity as a white, relatively prosperous gay man, they obviously constitute a limited subject—and, by no means incidentally, a limited group of readers. But there is no getting away from that identity, although to judge from the apologetic tone with which many of my white, relatively prosperous gay brothers in Academia refer to the racial and economic place they speak from, *they* at least can't be faulted for not trying. Everything I say is affected by the perspective that various circumstances have given me on whatever I say or do. It would be embarrassing to announce such an obvious truth were it not for the suspicion—by no means unfounded—that privileged white males tend to speak as if their assertions had some natural universality, taking place above the field of particular perspectives. At a gay and lesbian conference where I read part of Chapter 3, a lesbian colleague complained that my talk marginalized women. Since much of what I said had to do with gay men's sexuality and, more specifically, with gay men's love of the cock, her entirely accurate comment became entirely puzzling when voiced as a complaint. Why not object, more directly, to my talking about gay male sexuality at all? I wasn't necessarily "better" on gay male desire than she might have been on the same subject, and it is even conceivable that I might have been more acute than she if my topic had been lesbian sexuality. In any case, it is undeniable that my talk that day enjoyed, as it were, an explicit correspondence with my own sexual perspective and that *any* perspective, direct or vicarious, would be to some extent exclusionary.

Rather than deny or apologize for such exclusions,

we might more profitably acknowledge them and then try to see the unexpected ways in which an unavoidably limited "I" or "we" also speaks outside its particular perspective. My "we" in this book is constantly crossing over into the territory of other "we's." If I am resolutely excluded from lesbian sexuality in referring to the penis as a conscious source of erotic stimulation, lesbians, I would hope, will recognize themselves in a more socially positioned first-person plural—the "we" alluding to both gay men and lesbians as targets of homophobic aggression. I would also like to assume that, in spite of the enormous diversity among gay men, and taking into account the considerable historical variation in the very meaning of homosexual or gay, a black, economically disadvantaged gay man will find what I say about the homo-ness of gay men in Genet resonant with his own experience. The most varied, even antagonistic, identities meet transversely. These intersections of divergent lines of identity and experience give a pleasing instability to the "we" of this book. The instability, as readers will quickly recognize, is also intellectual: the positions I question have had considerable influence on my thinking about identity and sexuality, and so—theoretically as well as racially or economically—my "we" frequently defines a perspective that is at once mine and not mine.

This mobility should create a kind of community, one that can never be settled, whose membership is always shifting. It is also a community in which many straights should be able to find a place. Identity and sexual politics are not issues defined by particular sexual preferences. Still, many readers will find it useful to have an introduction to the particular gay contexts in which I discuss these issues. So I begin with an occasionally journalistic overview of "the gay presence" in America, which some of my gay readers may find unnecessary but which should help those less absorbed in today's queer scene to appreciate the irony in what I later speak of as "the gay absence." Furthermore, though I want to encourage thinking about gay specificity, I do not want to contribute to gay groupiness. The very people who object to being confined within a gay identity have formed a kind of ghetto of their own, based on the assumed superiority of queer culture to what is stigmatized as compulsory heterosexuality. If homosexuality is a privileged vehicle for homo-ness, the latter designates a mode of connectedness to the world that it would be absurd to reduce to sexual preference. An anticommunal mode of connectedness we might all share, or a new way of coming together: that, and not assimilation into already constituted communities, should be the goal of any adventure in bringing out, and celebrating, "the homo" in all of us.

1

The Gay Presence

Never before have gay men and women been so visible. If, as the citizens of Queer Nation have proclaimed, "we are everywhere," this should be understood as more than a defiant response to those who would sequester or, better, eradicate us; indeed, homophobic America itself appears to have an insatiable appetite for our presence. As a result, the social project inherent in the nineteenth-century invention of "the homosexual" can perhaps now be realized: visibility is a precondition of surveillance, disciplinary intervention, and, at the limit, gender-cleansing. The classification into character types of how people imagine and pursue their bodies' pleasures greatly reduced the heterogeneity of erotic behavior. A psychology of desire, as Foucault forcefully argued, drew those readable psychic maps on which human beings had to be assigned their places before territory could be occupied. Psychology in this argument *discovered* nothing; the questions it asked created the answers necessary to the social strategies that produced the questionnaire. Confession is a form of ventriloquism.

It is true that these strategies also had the reverse effect of producing, within the very entities mapped for control, resistance. The interiority of the strategically constructed target (the homosexual personality, for example) displayed unexpected resources for redrawing its own boundaries. This should not have come as a surprise. Interiority is a breeding ground not only for essences but also for a mobility incompatible with all essentializing definitions. To be a homosexual turned out to be something quite different from being the one targeted in the essentializing imperative. And yet, however shifty the target might be, a target had still become visible. From the point of view of the policing agents, that shiftiness was only an unfortunate but somewhat negligible by-product of their social blueprint. Once we agreed to be seen, we also agreed to being policed.

Given how ambiguous increased visibility can be, it is worth taking a closer look at both the agents and the modes of this new gay presence in America. On the one hand, there is—so it would seem—ample reason for celebration. Until recently, homosexuality was largely a coerced confession; we were to make ourselves visible so that we could be "treated"—therapeutically and juridically. Now the more we tell about ourselves, the more we are congratulated for being ourselves. Hardly a day goes by without the media focusing their appreciative beam on gay life—and gay death. In May 1993

Andrew Kopkind began a lead article in the *Nation* by proclaiming: "The gay moment is unavoidable. It fills the media, charges politics, saturates popular and elite culture." Kopkind's piece is in large part an impressive list of triumphs: "Broadway is bursting with gay plays, big book awards go to gay authors, even Hollywood is developing movies with gay themes"; gay and lesbian studies are on the curricula of hundreds of colleges; "out" gays have prominent positions in the professions; newspapers all over the country (including the *New York Times*) have openly gay columnists writing on gay issues; "TV is entering the gay nineties"; and, perhaps most impressive—especially after twelve years of homophobic Republicanism and "despite distressing backsliding"—we have "the first pro-gay White House."[1]

The point of Kopkind's clarifying piece was that the piece itself was not an exceptional event. A mere two months later, on July 5, the *Nation* neatly dubbed an issue almost entirely devoted to gay questions *The Queer Nation*. With its appointment of Andrew Sullivan as editor, the *New Republic* has the first out gay editor of a more or less mainstream national magazine, and on May 10, 1993, Sullivan published a special issue called *Straight America, Gay America*. The *New York Times* is almost overcompensating for its former reticence by giving startlingly generous news and editorial coverage to gay subjects. (The *Times* even complained editorially after the April 25, 1993, equal-rights march on Washington that most of the marchers seemed determined to give straight America respectable images of homosexuality.) And in its issue of June 21, 1993, the *New Yorker* carried both a short piece by the novelist and

New Yorker contributor Harold Brodkey announcing that he has AIDS and a much longer article on the murder of a millionaire corporate real-estate lawyer, David Schwartz, by a young hustler in a seedy Bronx motel. This piece was primarily a discussion of the closety atmosphere (homosexuality is ok as long as it remains invisible) at high-level corporate firms, an atmosphere at once uncongenial to the joyous self-outings celebrated by Kopkind and at least partially undercut and thereby readied for participation in those celebrations by the impersonal corporate outing performed by the reportage itself.

All the reports mentioned so far appeared during the few months preceding my account of them. The account represents nothing more than what I remember having recently read with some interest, and though more articles may have been published on gay issues during this time than during most other two-month periods, I don't think anyone would argue that in April and May of 1993 homosexuals were getting significantly more attention than they had in, say, the year or two before. After all, reports such as Kopkind's "The Gay Moment" give gays visibility by reporting on those areas—the arts, publishing, politics—in which gays are already visible. And I have barely mentioned what I know best: the flourishing academic industry of gay and lesbian studies. A recently published thick anthology of essays from this new interdisciplinary field includes a forbiddingly dense bibliography. There have been moments at some universities—Berkeley is one—when, to read a bulletin board of upcoming lectures and colloquia, a visitor might think that all the humanities departments had been merged into a single gay and lesbian studies program. Liberal straights respectfully attend lectures at which their own sexual preferences are confidently assigned to the erotic junkheap of compulsory heterosexuality—a practice into which millions of human beings have apparently been forced and from which they are now invited to liberate themselves.

A serious objection to my random survey of gay triumphs is of course that they are limited to elitist audiences. Indeed, the gay movement itself has been reproached for its easy victories—won by and over privileged groups in American society. How engrossed is the Heartland in the *New York Times,* Broadway, the *Nation,* the *New Republic,* the *New Yorker,* academic colloquia, and sympathetic reports on the MacNeil-Lehrer newshour? This brings us to the other side of the gay coin (though my argument will be that the victories themselves are in many ways a cop-out). Homophobic virulence in America has increased in direct proportion to the wider acceptance of homosexuals. The principal target of the religious right has been displaced from abortion to homosexuals. If our physical numbers were considerably less at the Republican than at the Democratic 1992 presidential convention, in another sense we were at least as present at the former as at the latter. It was widely reported that the Republican platform ended up more conservative than the party's leaders, although another way of putting it would be that the party's leaders were only too happy to let the fanatics do the dirty work—and that handing the convention over to Pat Robertson and his cohorts was an effective way of testing the viability of hate as a message in the

subsequent campaign. In any case, the Republican platform, arguing from within the Judeo-Christian tradition that it proudly advertised as the inspiration for its
viciousness, opposed same-sex marriages and adoption,
gave the party's support to the ban on gays in the military,
called for a law criminalizing the "deliberate" spread
of the HIV virus, and announced that condoms and
needle exchanges do not prevent AIDS.

How much homophobia in America has been or will
be affected by the Clinton presidency remains to be
seen. While it was probably a tactical mistake on Clinton's part to raise the issue of gays in the military during the first week of his presidency, his doing so certainly has added—hilariously and appallingly—to our
visibility (both real and fantasmatic). I was not alone
in being astonished by the prominence of shower rooms
in the erotic imagination of heterosexual American males.
Fear on the battlefield is apparently mild compared to
the terror of being "looked at" (and you know what
that means for most males). Men who refuse to believe
that women mean it when they say *no* have now begun
to express a visceral sympathy for the sexually besieged
woman. The *New York Times* reported on April 3,
1993, that a radar instructor who chose not to fly with
an openly gay sailor, Keith Meinhold, feared that Meinhold's "presence in the cockpit would distract him from
his responsibilities." The instructor "compared his 'shock'
at learning there was a gay sailor in his midst to a woman
discovering 'a man in the ladies' restroom.'" Note the
curious scatological transsexualism in our radar instructor's (let us hope momentary) identification of his cockpit
with a ladies' restroom.[2] In this strange scenario, the

potential gay attacker becomes the male intruder on female privacy, and the "original" straight man is meta-
morphosed, through another man's imagined sexual
attention, into the offended, harassed, or even violated
woman. Men's sympathy for the women they harass can
go no further, although gay men are bound to be an-
gered by the scenario as yet another example of straight
men's untroubled assumptions that gays find them sexually irresistible—an assumption voiced in recent months
just as often by jowly retired admirals as by more or
less cute twenty-year-olds. Shower-room rape or forced
fellatio are of course not the only scourges to be visited
on the military with the lifting of the ban. In the ani-
mated cartoon of our military leaders' and portly sena-
tors' fantasies, the HIV virus, even if gay soldiers remain virtuously, stoically, between their own sheets,
will make its insidious way from cot to cot in the erotically suffocating and disease-breeding space of homo-
and heterosexual military cohabitation.

The compromise policy that was finally adopted
("Don't ask, don't tell, don't pursue") suggests that
even more dangerous than the presence of gays in the
military (everyone knows they're already there) is the
prospect of their saying they're there. In what way?
The homoeroticism inherent in military life certainly
risks being exposed to those who would at once deny
and enjoy it when self-confessed homos from within the
ranks go public. But perhaps the most serious danger
in gay Marines being open about their gayness is that
they might begin, like some of their gay civilian brothers, to play at being Marines. Not that they would
make fun of the Marines. On the contrary: they may

find ways of being so Marine-like that they will no longer be "real" Marines. D. A. Miller has a marvelous passage in *Bringing Out Roland Barthes* on "the different priorities of the macho straight male body and the so-called gym body of the gay male culture": "Even the most macho gay image tends to modify cultural fantasy about the male body if only by suspending the main response that the armored body seems developed to induce: if this is still *the body that can fuck you, etc.,* it is no longer—quite the contrary—*the body you don't fuck with.*"[3] And Jacques Lacan, in an analogous if considerably less celebratory observation, notes that virile displays always seem feminine.[4] What passes for the real thing self-destructs from within its theatricalized replication. The imaginary negates the real to which it purportedly adheres. In imagining what he presumably already is (both gay and a Marine), the gay Marine may learn the invaluable lesson that *identity is not serious* (as if what he is imitating never existed before it was imitated).

Nothing is more inimical to military life than that lesson. So the major (and as far as I'm concerned desirable) menace of gays who speak their gayness is less to the straight soldiers and sailors whose readiness for discipline and combat would, it is feared, crumble in the debilitating excitement of the gay confessional, but rather to the gay soldiers and sailors themselves. The military might lose them as they begin to move about in their roles, to voice and to advertise their versatile (ever hardening and ever melting) masculinity in a context where masculinity is not supposed to move. The gay soldier letting out his gayness may begin to see its theatricalities as incompatible with the monolithic theatricality of military masculinity. Gays might then begin to abandon the armed forces by the thousands—which could sap the morale of their deserted straight comrades and furnish recruits for a new type of antimilitarism (yet to be defined), one somewhere "between" or "outside" both pacifism and guerrilla terrorism.

Nothing has made gay men more visible than AIDS. If we are looked at more than we have ever been looked at before—for the most part proudly by ourselves, sympathetically or malevolently by straight America—it is because AIDS has made us *fascinating*. While apprehensiveness about HIV led thousands of gay men to become habitués of health clubs, the "gym body of the gay male culture" can no longer be merely admired in the club's floor-to-ceiling mirrors; now every blemish is scrutinized for a fearsome resemblance to *molluscum contagiosum* or, worse, KS, and a scrutiny of body bulk and muscle definition may send us rushing to the weight machine rather than back to the free weights. And we have, sadly, become used to more or less discreet, more or less urgent questions in the eyes of those who don't dare put the questions into words: is he HIV-positive? What symptoms does he have? How long before . . .? Thanks largely to television and movies, the entire country has been able to take in (while of course distancing itself from) images of our wasted bodies. The normal fear of homosexuality has been promoted to a compelling terror as a secret fantasy becomes a public spectacle: the spectacle of men dying from what I called in "Is the Rectum a Grave?" the suicidal ecstasy of taking their sex like a woman.

In the face of all this, there is, we might at first think,

something mysterious about gay exuberance. As the epidemic spreads, as more and more of our friends die, as the medical establishment finally begins to suggest that the antiviral therapy it has been pushing is ineffective, gays have never been gayer. In the early days of the epidemic, many of us adopted part of the fundamentalist argument that AIDS was the not entirely undeserved consequence of the unbridled poppered promiscuity of the 1970s, of our perverse preference for five or ten partners in the bathhouse over the one-and-only in the drug-free privacy of a suburban home. Monogamy continues to have its appeal (the demand for legalized gay marriages testifies to that), but promiscuity has also made its insidious way back. Sex clubs are thriving (and, perhaps related to this, the incidence of HIV has risen among young queers, many of whom apparently think AIDS is a generational disease).

In addition to this renewed sexual energy, there were the joyous turnouts all over the country, just a few days before my writing these words, for Lesbian and Gay Pride Day, 1993 (and just before this book goes to press, the celebrations and media coverage of the twenty-fifth anniversary of Stonewall). It is as if AIDS, the devastating depletor of the body's energies, had energized the survivors. Look at us: We're still alive. We won't be made to feel guilty, we're having sex—lots of it—again. Look at us: We demand the rights and privileges that you enjoy. We demand a future without discrimination even as AIDS makes us wonder how much of a future we have. Rather than make us shameful about who we are and how we desire, AIDS has helped more of us to come out than ever before—as if to help you, straight

America, fight the terrifying fantasies "legitimated" by AIDS with the knowledge that we are already your neighbors and that our sins can be as ordinary, as unworthy of fantasy-fabulation, as yours. Look at us: We're not only here, everywhere at your side, but also everywhere in history, in neglected works and figures but also in the subtexts of the masterpieces of western civilization.

In fact, no one can stop looking. But we might wonder if AIDS, in addition to transforming gay men into infinitely fascinating taboos, has also made it *less dangerous* to look. For, our projects and our energies notwithstanding, others may think of themselves as watching us disappear. The heightened visibility conferred on gay men by AIDS is the visibility of imminent death, of a promised invisibility. Straight America can rest its gaze on us, let us do our thing over and over in the media, because what our attentive fellow citizens see is the pathos and impotence of a doomed species.

Two recent reports—which once again made gays highly visible in the media—support my sense of the intimate connection between our remarkable presence in America today and the absence with which the nation may be rewarded for allowing the presence. In February 1993 the National Research Council made public a study asserting that the AIDS epidemic will have little impact on the life of most Americans. Since AIDS is concentrated among homosexuals, drug users, the poor, and the undereducated—what the council calls "socially marginalized groups" with "little economic, political, and social power"—the epidemic will have minimal effect on "the structures and directions of [American] social institutions."[5] The *New York Times* article summarizing the report was, on the one hand, a caricature. By highlighting the conclusions just summarized, it suggested a heartless and vicious document. In fact, this 300-page study is in many ways a model of humane objectivity. Though the general sociological discourse of which it is a part prevents it from being explicitly prescriptive, it speaks with concern of the "psychological burdens" borne by those who are stigmatized as a result of HIV infection,[6] and it warns of the potential infringement, by government, of the civil rights of HIV-positive people in economically deprived and politically powerless communities. On the other hand, the *Times* article accurately summarizes what might be called the report's unconscious, where irrationality and even ferocity are in direct proportion to the report's neutrality and its consistently maintained distance from the explosive medical, sexual, and political questions it raises.

That unconscious operates throughout the report to transform HIV disease into a geographically and socially defined and confined epidemic. It thrives in communities that are already "islands of illness," where there is already a "synergism of plagues." The council's study of New York City in particular reveals a "chilling epidemological fact: HIV/AIDS is but one in an overlapping cluster of epidemics." The conflation of AIDS with other diseases endemic to "areas in which economically impoverished members of ethnic minorities live" is effected by a significant slippage in the report's definition of the HIV-infected population, a slippage that might seem authorized by the actual progression of the disease. "At its outset," the report notes in its general findings, "HIV disease settled among socially disvalued groups, and as the epidemic has progressed, AIDS has increasingly been an affliction of people who have little economic, political, and social power." Here the council could be thought of as allying itself with those AIDS activists who protest against what they see as a disproportionate amount of AIDS care and money going to middle-class white gay men—to the detriment of the growing numbers of HIV cases among inner-city minorities. But the council, with its nonprescriptive bias, makes no such protest, and its emphasis on the movement of HIV from "socially devalued groups" (presumably gay men) to people without power works to facilitate a socially and politically convenient view of AIDS as an *immobilized epidemic.* The choice of New York City as the one area studied in detail helps somewhat to justify this view, since a zip-code analysis of HIV in the city reveals that the epidemic is "concentrated in a small number of communities, which are in large part insulated from the rest of the city." Like other diseases in the synergism of plagues, "AIDS cases are also concentrated in zones of urban poverty, poor health care, drug addiction, and social disintegration."[7]

By the end of the report, HIV (which is "not a city-wide disease" in New York), having been immobilized, can therefore be seen as having comparatively little impact on American society. It is not a question of denying the validity of the zip-code charts; the question concerns the political function and usefulness of that (never explicitly stated) "therefore." Because the report appears to have been written by people who believe that the only question to be asked about a conclusion is whether it is statistically valid, the report can remain blithely ignorant of its conclusion's prescriptive force. The closest we come to a gap in the barrier protecting the report's unconscious is when it announces: "HIV/AIDS will 'disappear,' not because, like smallpox, it has been eliminated, but because those who continue to be affected by it are socially invisible, beyond the sight and attention of the majority population." Not only does this do away with the thousands of gay men who, far from remaining beyond sight and attention, live and work in the midst of the general population and, what is worse, can usually not be distinguished from it; it also suggests that HIV will really disappear (without the quotation marks) only when the afflicted populations have themselves been eliminated by the disease. The social and geographic mobility of the majority of HIV carriers can go unmentioned because that mobility is irrelevant to the ghettoization of the epidemic.

What the writers of the report do not consider is that the decimation by disease of certain minority populations is itself the major impact of HIV on American society. The fantasizing of those populations as "socially invisible" authorizes the wishful redefinition of American society as white, middle-class, and heterosexual; AIDS becomes the means for making that wish come true. In sum, the council's prediction of the impact of AIDS on the United States is drawn not so much from research leading up to that prediction as it is from the very content of the prediction (when you already eliminate large groups, a population can then be called free of AIDS). If this even-handed, humane document can be considered evil, that is because of its implicit but no less powerful prescription to the makers of American policy: it is not necessary or even desirable to do anything about fighting an epidemic that may miraculously transform a social desire for the invisibility of certain groups into a social reality. In time, AIDS will fully realize its potential as a politically and morally hygienic agent.

Such implicit prescriptions become especially persuasive if we take into account three considerations that have in all probability been crucial in the formulation of government policies on AIDS. First of all, while medical researchers tell us that they have learned more about HIV in a dozen or so years than has ever been known about a major disease in a comparable period of time, they also say they are not much closer to effective therapy than they were in 1982. Second, contrary to earlier fears, and in spite of a dramatic rise recently in heterosexual transmissions of HIV, the non-IV heterosexual population in the United States has remained largely free of the virus. If drugusers get points for being straight, those are quickly withdrawn because they do use drugs and, to boot, are mostly poor. Despite what the National Research Council at times appears to suggest, the contributions of drug-free gay men to mainstream society can be convincingly demonstrated—but not much of a case can be made for a black poor single female drug addict and her infected children. How could they possibly contribute to the "structures and directions" of American social institutions or, more grandly, to western civilization? For all the marginal and useless compassion they elicit, they are a drag on our national resources. Only a nation firmly committed to the democratic ideal—that society is responsible for at least creating the conditions for the well-being of all its citizens—would consider that it has an obligation to save infected drugusers. A country (I mean the United States) that has long resisted the idea of free vaccinations for all children can hardly be said to entertain such impractical notions. Alone among the industrially developed countries, we act as if we'd rather die from lack of medical treatment than have our ideological purity sullied by something referred to with revulsion as "socialized medicine." As medical costs soar, however, and as more and more middle-class people discover the sacrifices their loyalty to unmodified free enterprise may entail, we are at last becoming sympathetic to the old concept of universal health care—although, as seen in the objections of employers to pay for health insurance, not as sympathetic as we are to the cash-flow problems of small business. Thus, against much resistance and with many concessions to business and the health industry, America, just short of the year 2000, has timidly put one foot in the twentieth century with its consideration of the Clinton health-care proposals.

And the third consideration behind government policy on AIDS: homosexuals may constitute a much smaller percentage of the population than had been thought. A study released shortly after that of the National Research Council estimated the gay male population in the United States at approximately 1 percent (far below the 10 percent suggested years ago by the Kinsey Report). The *New York Times* reported this finding on page one—without, however, informing its readers (at least not until a few days later, on an inside page) that pollsters went to the homes of those interviewed and, while promising confidentiality, asked for each respondent's social security number and name of employer before recording his sexual preference. It could of course be argued that when you're counting queers, even a hundredth of 1 percent can be a scary figure. Unlike racism, homophobia is entirely a response to an internal possibility. Though racism and homophobia both include powerful projective energies, the projections are quite different. A white racist projects onto blacks some lurid sexual fantasies of his own, but essentially his version of "the nature of blacks"—not only as (secretly envied) sexual animals but also as lazy, prone to violence, intellectually deficient—is a response to what he sees as an external threat, a threat to personal safety, economic security, and the achievements of white civilization. Blacks are a dangerous and inferior race, and they may destroy us. But not even racists could ever fear that blacks will seduce them into becoming black. Homophobia, on the other hand, is precisely that: to let gays be open about their gayness, to give them equal rights, to allow them to say who they are and what they want, is to risk being recruited.

The pleasure promised by that recruitment must be very great indeed in order to offset the fear of possible death from AIDS after the recruitment is successful. Of course, to the extent that gay male sexuality has been identified with an imagined version of female sexuality, that danger has always existed. AIDS, like syphilis in the nineteenth century, merely legitimates a fantasy of both gay and female sexuality as diseased, indeed fatal. To argue for the strong possibility of recruitment in such circumstances is almost to acknowledge a suicidal impulse, and can, I think, be explained only by the power of a promised pleasure—a pleasure whose power the straight man already knows. In his curious conviction that thousands of heterosexuals could easily be converted to the homosexual cause, the homophobic male must be "remembering" a lost jouissance (that is, female sexuality as a male body has in fantasy experienced it). Women are probably perceived as being too different from men to hold out the prospect of a man becoming a woman; that ambiguous privilege falls to gay males, in whom straight men can more easily recognize the otherness in themselves. Because homophobia may be this fearful excitement at the prospect of becoming what one already is, the numerical strength of homosexuals is, in a sense, irrelevant. One gay man rumored to be furtively cruising the toilets deep in a distant province of a nation otherwise totally successful in its genocidal campaign against gays would be enough to hold up, for his appalled and expectant countrymen, the mirror in which they could not escape recognizing their already recruited selves.

But the elimination of blacks would, at least temporarily, soothe racist fears. Some other people would undoubtedly have to be found to give historical plausibility to the destructive impulses that fed the fear of blacks. Still, at least as far as blacks themselves are concerned, the threat they pose is gone once they disappear. Rather, they are not incarnations of that threat, whereas the threat of homosexuality does not lie in the characteristics attributed to it: it is exactly identical with just being homosexual. No other group could carry the menace of homosexuality without turning out to *be* a homosexual group. (Koreans would not become blacks if we began projecting onto them the fantasy burdens now borne by blacks.)

And yet precisely because homosexuals cannot be eliminated, the need to pursue them becomes all the more urgent. The illusion that they are other, that they exist only out there, must at all costs be maintained. Any slackening of homophobic virulence could be seen as an inadmissable recognition of the futility of the pursuit. AIDS is a great boon to the cause: it never stops killing (it might even be counted on to keep killing the damnably inevitable gays of future generations), and the homophobe can even relax somewhat as the miracle virus does his work for him. If the extinction of gays as a "species" is thorough, homophobia itself may no longer be necessary. Inasmuch as homophobia is itself the sign of the ineradicability of homosexuality, however, it must remain. It must always be there, on guard against that to which it testifies.

2

The Gay Absence

Gays and lesbians have certainly been working to make themselves visible—but how they have been doing it is at least as ambiguous as straight America's motives in tolerating, even encouraging, this unprecedented visibility. If we are indeed everywhere, it is by no means clear who the "we" is. As the battle for gay rights is engaged in more and more American communities, and as the battleground becomes more and more spacious (from the struggle over what we have the right to do in the privacy of our bedrooms to the public arenas of the workplace, the military, the schools, and the church), what it means just to be gay has become surprisingly problematic. Never before in the history of minority groups struggling for recognition and equal treatment has there been an analogous attempt, on the part of any such group, to make itself unidentifiable even as it demands to be recognized.

I want to examine a paradox as disturbing as it is stimulating: many of the most articulate members of an oppressed community have defined the acceptance of that community's visibility as an acknowledgment of its invisibility. In its confident assertion of omnipresence, the slogan "We are everywhere" appears to be saying: "Look around and you'll find us in all the places to which you thought you had denied us access." But the slogan could also have a quite different gloss: "Look around and you'll never find us *because* we are everywhere. And even if we do the most outrageous things to make ourselves recognizable—even if I kiss my male lover's mouth in the middle of your straight suburban mall—we will remain unlocatable." Invisibly visible, unlocatably everywhere: if the gay presence is threatened by absence, it is not only because of the secret (or not so secret) intentions of those who are fascinated by gays, or even as a result of the devastating work of AIDS, but also because gays have been de-gaying themselves in the very process of making themselves visible.

We can approach what I have in mind from different perspectives. First of all, I can't be oppressed if I can't be found. Unidentifiability is an act of defiance, and the confrontational nature of gays' self-erasure has been clear since the 1960s. Nearly a decade before Foucault analyzed the disciplinary designs behind the classification of perversions, the sociologist Mary McIntosh spoke of "the social labeling of persons as deviant" as "a mechanism of social control."[1] The gay liberationists of the early 1970s, as Steven Epstein notes, repudiated "the notion of 'the homosexual' as a distinct type . . . in favor of a left Freudian view of human sexuality as 'polymorphously perverse.'"[2] In "The End of the Homosexual?", the last chapter of his 1971 book, *Homosexual: Oppression and Liberation,* Dennis Altman welcomed the promise of a "new human" for whom the distinction between masculinity and femininity would be irrelevant.[3] That the 1970s also witnessed a phenomenal growth of gay communities was perhaps the result of a dilemma aptly summarized by Epstein: "How do you protest a socially imposed categorization, except by organizing around the category?"[4] Foucault also spoke of the "reverse discourse" in which "homosexuality began to speak in its own behalf, to demand that its legitimacy or 'naturality' be acknowledged, often in the same vocabulary, using the same categories by which it was medically disqualified," thus challenging the power structures responsible for its creation.[5]

Now you see us, now you don't. Gay history from the time homosexuality was invented as a category could be written in terms of this disappearing and reappearing act—almost as if homosexuality were nothing but a reaction, the responses of a social group to its own invention. The type of resistance Foucault mentioned does not exactly challenge the notion of a homosexual identity. In spite of the oppressive intent in the social manipulations of the category, "homosexuality" was also received as an opportunity for self-fashioning. Even if the targeted men and women forged their own identity and culture in "the same categories by which [homosexuality] was medically disqualified," the homosexual personality could also be experienced as a psychic enrichment. Today we tend to lament the rigidifying of acts of same-sex physical intimacy into an "inner essence," but the new (if they were new) psychic structures thus created could also lend legitimacy and dignity to the acts themselves. It is, after all, not as if those acts were viewed indifferently by earlier western societies. Sodomy, that statutory "abominable and detestable crime against nature," defined perverts and inverts; their gathering together as a politically militant group was unthinkable. The sodomite had no self-defense since, as a sodomite, he was nothing but the acts designated by the term. "Homosexuality," on the other hand, provided a context in which sodomy could begin to signify in new ways. The sodomite had no case to make for his sexual practices; the homosexual personality, by psychologizing such practices and integrating its sexuality into the structures of a demonstrably viable social self, could begin to make a persuasive case for legitimation. The invention of the homosexual may have been the precondition of sexual liberation in that the homosexual essence partially desexualizes (and thereby sanitizes or domesticates) the very acts that presumably called the essence into being. It is hardly surprising that—as Freud testifies when, with some irritation, he refers to the homosexuals of his time thinking of themselves as an elite—something like gay pride, far from being a result of the Stonewall riot in 1969 (in response to the police raid of a Greenwich Village gay disco), seems to have been contemporaneous with the actual "creation" of homosexuality.

If, as I have been suggesting, gay pride has become something much more ambiguous, it is because we have become suspicious not merely of specific identities, but of identity itself. Foucault's notion that homosexuality has only been around since 1870, however questionable it may be historically,[6] has given a crucial, probably irreversible turn to our thinking: in asserting the historical contingency of homosexuality, he invites us to question the entire system of gendered binary oppositions of which homosexuality is only one term. Far more significant than the rightness or wrongness of the dating is the related claim, made by some of Foucault's followers, that just about everything we take for granted about sexuality and sex, even the very differences between the sexes, may be to a significant degree learned, and that to unlearn it all may be our greatest political challenge.

Homosexual–heterosexual, masculinity–femininity, man–woman: the only proper way of thinking about these categories, many now think, is to investigate their cultural determinants. The dating of homosexuality was a momentous event because it initiated the study of how culture regulates identity. In a recent volume of essays on the controversy between social constructionism and essentialism, Edward Stein defines constructionism as "the view that there are no objective, culture-independent categories of sexual orientation—no one is, independent of a culture, a heterosexual or homosexual."[7] As this suggests, the most radical element in constructionist studies is to question the given or natural status of *heterosexuality*. No longer the stable norm from which same-sex desire deviates (so that the problem is always how the norm was abandoned and how it may be recaptured), heterosexuality, as Lee Edelman puts it, constitutes "a psychic economy that defines itself *against* the historically available category of the 'homosexual.'"[8] The latter would be the invention necessary to keep the always shaky construction of heterosexuality intact. Not only did homosexuals find their existence and identity within the categories from which they had been fashioned by straight society; they were also a distinctively heterosexual fantasy, the internally excluded difference that cements heterosexual identity.

Does this mean that lurking behind heterosexuality is a more "original" homosexuality, a same-sex sex drive that the invention of homosexuality helps to repress? That we may be inclined to answer this question in the negative—or, more effectively, simply to dismiss the question—indicates how far we have come from defending homosexuality on the basis of a presumably natural bisexuality or, even better, polymorphously perverse sexuality. Psychoanalysis has been of great service in the mounting of these defenses. Freud spoke of the repression of a primary bisexuality in all human beings in the normative maturation of desire (and its "satisfactory" climax in genital heterosexuality), and recent critics have emphasized the extent to which, according to Freud himself, the heterosexual denouement of infantile drives is a fragile, defensive, inescapably neurotic resolution to the "series of psychic traumas" that constitute the Oedipus complex.[9] But most of these liberalizing arguments leave intact the fundamental homosexual-heterosexual dichotomy. Since, as Judith Butler has pointed out, bisexuality is conceptualized by Freud in terms of feminine and masculine "dispositions" that have heterosexual aims (it is in desiring like a woman that a boy sees his father as an object of sexual love), bisexuality is simply "the coincidence of two heterosexual desires within a single psyche."[10] As for the polymorphously perverse, while it values free-floating sexuality, its promoters do not attack the idea of a maturational process, where identities are constructed. That process remains as a legitimate description of psychic history; what changes is the most desirable holding position.[11]

We have become far more ambitious: we want to study the effects, and question the necessity, of *all* gendered oppositions. Philosophically, this means deconstructing the assumption that, as Michael Warner puts it, "gender is the phenomenology of difference itself."[12] That assumption has been shown to operate as the epistemological given even in the purportedly neutral descriptions of the natural sciences. Bonnie Spanier's feminist analysis of the field of molecular biology has uncovered "inaccurate and masculinist superimpositions of Western sex/gender systems onto organisms at the cellular and molecular levels." In tracing "the propensity for and tenacity of genderizing nongendered beings" (for instance, bacteria), Spanier convincingly argues that "the scientific definition of sex—the exchange of genetic material between organisms—is confused with the cultural sense of sex—a sexual act between a male and a female in which the male is the initiator who makes the sex act happen and who donates genetic material while the female is the passive recipient."[13] Such demonstrations lend credibility to Monique Wittig's claim—which we might at first consider to be as ideologically biased as the culture she criticizes—that "heterosexuality is always already there within all mental categories." It is "*the* social contract . . . a political regime." Beginning with Aristotle's *Politics,* in which the first two examples of "those which are ineffective without each other [and therefore] must be unified in a pair" are male and female and ruler and ruled, the heterosexual relationship "has been the parameter of all hierarchical relations."[14]

What Wittig calls the "straight mind" would be more easily recognizable as a political regime if she admitted a difference between heterosexual and heterosexist. But she sees the category of the heterosexual itself as a political arrangement. It is not that we have been ruled by bad heterosexuals; the need to be identified as heterosexual is already a heterosexist position. Wittig gives some plausibility to her claim by defining that need in materialist terms: heterosexuality stabilizes class oppression as a permanent fact of human nature. It creates a ruling class exempt from historical vicissitudes (which frequently redistribute power: from the nobility to the bourgeoisie, from the bourgeoisie to the proletariat). "Men" and "women" in Wittig's radical argument are political creations designed to give a biological mandate to social arrangements in which one group of human beings oppresses another. Relations among people are always constructed, and the question to be asked is not which ones are the most natural, but rather what interests are served by each construction. Thus, glossing Wittig's gloss of Aristotle, we could say that she sees the first example in the *Politics* as both dictated by and legitimating the second: the case of male and female naturalizes the relation between ruler and ruled as one that must take place. The ruled is as ineffective without the ruler as the implicitly ruled female is without a male ruler; an elementary linguistic axiom (without "ruled" we wouldn't know what "ruler" means, just as "no" gives sense to "yes") is surreptitiously promoted to a political axiom, that the domination of one group by another is a necessary social structure.

The most interesting (and, given our religion of diversity, courageous) aspect of this argument is Wittig's suspicion of difference. She goes further than protesting the equation of gender with the phenomenology of difference itself. The "different-other" is always—would anyone call this a coincidence?—in the inferior position: "Men are not different, whites are not different, nor are the masters. But the blacks, as well as the slaves, are." She concludes: "The concept of difference has nothing ontological about it. It is only the way that the masters interpret a historical situation of domination. The function of difference is to mask at every level the conflicts of interest, including ideological ones."[15]

The straight mind valorizes difference. While you obviously don't have to be straight to think straight, Wittig's association of heterosexuality with a hierarchical view of difference could be defended psychoanalytically. Kenneth Lewes, writing from a Freudian perspective, argues that a primarily heterosexual orientation of desire is, for the little boy, the result of a flight to the father following a horrified retreat from women.[16] Male heterosexuality would be a *traumatic* privileging of difference. Moreover, to the extent that the perception of difference is, for all human subjects, traumatizing, it is perhaps necessarily accompanied by a defensively hierarchical attribution of value. Wittig's remark that the different is always in an inferior position would be justified by this originally self-protective devaluation of a threatening otherness. The cultural consolidation of heterosexuality is grounded in its more fundamental, nonreflective construction as the compulsive repetition of a traumatic response to difference.

The straight mind might be thought of as a sublimation of this privileging of difference. If its achievements in the history of civilization are far more impressive, and civilizing, than Wittig would allow, it has also developed, and made "natural," a system of thinking in which differences are maintained largely through a persistent habit of hierarchical placement. If it is difficult, within this system, to think of differences nonantagonistically, it is because, as I suggested, antagonism is bound up in the very origins of differential perception. Dialectical thinking and dialogue seek to effect reconciliations between opposed terms, but these reconciliations may require the transcendence or even the annihilation of the differential terms. The straight mind thinks alone; as the history of philosophy demonstrates, the thinking of distinctions (that is, philosophical thought) performatively establishes the distinctness, and the distinction, of the thinker. Distinctiveness and distinction: the philosophical performance can't help conferring value on itself, for that value is the very sign of its distinctness and its defense against an "outside" dominated by the assumption that the world, the real, can be an object of thought, can be described, measured, known. So the tonal sign of the straight mind is its seriousness: differences are validated by the thinker's demonstration of how seriously he takes his own statements—and this may be the only validation we can give to the philosophic myth of truth.

It could of course be objected that the straight mind is nothing less than the human mind. Rather than argue for the truth-value of Wittig's argument (which would be to validate it by the very criteria she implicitly attributes to straight thinking), let's assign it the heuristic value of opening up a new line of inquiry. Is there another way of thinking? Could we authenticate the idea of the straight mind by demonstrating the possibility of thinking outside it? To a certain extent, those designated as homosexuals have acquiesced in the identity thrust upon them. But even that passivity creates a certain divorce from the straight mind that has invented them, clears a space, first of all, for reflection on the heterosexual identity from which they are being excluded. More interestingly, the possibility arises of enacting an alternative to the straight mind. For we are in effect being summoned—unintentionally, to be sure, and the cue provided is still merely etymological—to rethink economies of human relations on the basis of homo-ness, of sameness. Is there a specificity in homo-ness, or, in other terms, how is sameness different?

By this question we do risk repeating the operation I've just criticized with nothing more than a shift in the privileged term of difference. Instead of making the privileging of difference the superior term in the homo-heterosexual opposition we are simply putting it in the inferior position and replacing it with a different structure of relationality. Yet there may be no other way to resist the reduction of homosexuality to the system that would put it down. My argument is that by not accepting and radically reworking the different identity of sameness—by rejecting the whole concept of identity—we risk participating in the homophobic project that wants to annihilate us. Only an emphasis on the specifics of sameness can help us to avoid collaborating in the disciplinary tactics that would make us invisible. In other words, there *is* a "we." But in our anxiety to convince straight society that we are only some malevolent invention and that we can be, like you, good soldiers, good parents, and good citizens, we seem bent on suicide. By erasing our identity we do little more than reconfirm its inferior position within a homophobic system of differences.

Wittig, having laid the basis for precisely the kind of adventure I propose, nonetheless derails that adventure by refusing to grant any sexual specificity to gayness. Her suspicion of difference is so rigorously maintained that she lends herself—unfortunately, for her work is important—to charges of metaphysical quackery. She recasts homosexuality outside the parameters of sexual difference. She is less concerned to collapse the opposition between heterosexual and homosexual than to deconstruct the difference between the sexes that biologically authenticates that opposition. Heterosexuality does not merely privilege different-sex desire over same-sex desire; it promotes the myth that there really is a difference between the sexes. The truly villainous categories are "man" and "woman"; within that opposition heterosexuality grounds itself as natural and stigmatizes homosexuality as a narcissistic rejection of the other. Thus, "the refusal to become (or to remain) heterosexual always meant to refuse to become a man or a woman, consciously or not." Lesbianism has to be redefined in terms far more radical than those provided by the anodyne notion of a "lesbian continuum," which merely allows the category to cover a broad spectrum of relations (sexual and nonsexual) among women. Wittig, in a totally logical and, for many, insane move, asserts: "it would be incorrect to say that lesbians associate, make love, live with women, for 'woman' has meaning only in heterosexual systems of thought and heterosexual economic systems. Lesbians are not women."[17]

What are they, then? In an interesting, largely sympathetic discussion of Wittig, Judith Butler notes that for Wittig only by "effectively lesbianizing the entire world can the compulsory order of heterosexuality be destroyed." Somehow homosexuality is "radically unconditioned by heterosexual norms," and related to its opposite only as an act of protest.[18] Foucault's "reverse discourse" is cut off from that which, for Foucault, made it possible: the production and marginalizing of a homosexual identity by heterosexual power structures. Wittig sees lesbians as socially conditioned only in the sense that heterosexual society compels them to discover their autonomy, and so lesbianism comes perilously close to being a product of nature. We could even say that nature is also hidden at the other extreme. Man *and* woman are heterosexual inventions for Wittig, but who or what, exactly, were the heterosexuals who invented them? The answer has to be "man," since the categories of sex, according to Wittig, were created in order to ensure male domination over women.

Then this means that there were men preceding the creation of man. Who were these men, what were they like? If there were "men" before heterosexual "man," what could have motivated them to become that man, except an oppressive intention characterizing that which they had not yet become? At both ends of history, there is something ahistorical: the "afterwards" of the homosexual protest and, more obscurely, the inconceivable "before" necessary to create "man" and "woman" (without that "before," the categories have to be given, natural). Indeed, for Wittig the history of man and woman is fundamentally an ontological fall. Gender seeks to divide originally undivided Being.[19] There are therefore no attributes to be sought in sameness; Wittig is as uninterested in a gay or lesbian identity as she is in femininity or female writing. Homosexuality in her thought is unconditioned because it is a metaphysical category.

So extraordinarily privileged, homosexuality becomes empirically unrecognizable. To say that it designates same-gender desire would be to admit the very categories Wittig tells us to destroy. Finally, she sees very well that the ultimate refuge of those categories is the human body. Particular cultural definitions of man and woman can be challenged without the categories themselves being put into question. Even the repudiation of all notions of masculinity and femininity can leave the distinction between male and female standing. An irreducible bodily binary, it could be said, has been used as the pretext for factitious, ideologically motivated distinctions between feminine and masculine. This would be sensible, but Wittig is, conceptually and politically, far more ambitious. She argues that the body is never merely given; it too is constructed. And the construction is primarily linguistic; the sexual hierarchizing of the body by language is the precondition for the entire system of sexual differences. As Butler puts it: "That penis, vagina, breasts, and so forth, are *named* sexual parts is both a restriction of the erogenous body to those parts and a fragmentation of the body as a whole."[20] Heterosexuality will rise again and again from the ashes of our cultural struggles as long as the heterosexual body remains intact. Thus the violence of Wittig's fiction, in which bodies are (at least textually) torn apart, dismembered, so that they may be configured and eroticized anew. Wittig could be thought of as a Foucauldian warrior, far more guerrilla-like (to borrow the title of one of her books) in taking up Foucault's cause of a new economy of the body's pleasures than Foucault himself ever was. Wittig the martyr, ready to sacrifice her own body to the logic of her lesbian passion: at an incomparably absurd and poignant moment during a lecture at Vassar College, Wittig, asked whether she had a vagina, answered no. That nasty question instantaneously created Wittig as a woman (thus condensing centuries of heterosexual culture's work); her answer, however, just as rapidly reinscribed "lesbian" on her body, effectively erasing the cultural sign and stigma of "woman."

It is doubtful that Wittig herself realizes how politically nonviable such self-erasures are. Judith Butler's *Gender Trouble* is a brilliant attempt to fit some of the radical aspects of Wittig's thought into a workable political program. Echoing Wittig, Butler asks: "To what extent does the category of women achieve stability and coherence only in the context of the heterosexual matrix?" Recognizing the importance of how we think about the body for any successful resistance to the assignment of gendered identities, Butler cites feminist critics of the field of molecular biology whose work suggests that "gendered meanings frame the hypothesis and the reasoning of those biomedical inquiries that seek to establish 'sex' for us as it is prior to the cultural meanings that it acquires." If even the mundane fact of sex assignment never operates independently of cultural determinants, then we are justified in rethinking the ways in which our bodies are culturally mapped, and in particular how their boundaries are drawn. The description of bodies in terms of binary sex depends on "the cultural discourse that takes external genitalia to be the sure signs of sex," a discourse that itself serves "the social organization of sexual reproduction through the construction of the clear and unequivocal identities and positions of sexed bodies with respect to each other." Citing Mary Douglas' argument in *Purity and Danger* that "the body is a model that can stand for any bounded system" and that "its boundaries can represent any boundaries which are threatened or precarious," Butler emphasizes the dangers for the social system of "permeable bodily boundaries." Homosexual sex—especially anal sex between men—is a threatening "boundary-trespass," a site of danger and pollution for the social system represented synechdochally by the body.[21]

Any activity or condition that exposes the permeability of bodily boundaries will simultaneously expose the factitious nature of sexual differences as they are postulated within the heterosexual matrix. All this is consistent with Wittig's devaluation of difference and her interest in "exploding" the heterosexually sexed body in order to experiment with new ways of being a body and, correlatively, with new cultural orders. Butler separates herself from Wittig in her recognition that the lesbian (and gay male?) body cannot be constructed entirely outside the heterosexuality it would subvert. In insisting on a subversive "resignifying" of heterosexuality rather than its "thoroughgoing displacement," Butler relocates homosexuality itself within the field of cultural politics. So she looks favorably on those gay and lesbian discourses in which terms such as queens, bitches, femmes, girls, dyke queer, and fag are prominent, since they effectively redeploy and destabilize the derogatory categories of homosexual identity.

Within this program of subversive appropriation and parodistic redeployment of the dominant culture's styles and discourse, drag takes on extraordinary value. In performing a dissociation "not only between sex and performance, but sex and gender, and gender and performance," drag presumably reveals the original gendered body as itself performative. *"In imitating gender, drag implicitly reveals the imitative structure of gender itself—as well as its contingency"* (Butler's emphasis). It invites us to free our subsequent gender experience from what we might have thought of, until the moment of drag's liberating lesson, as an immutable primary gender identification. In *Gender Trouble,* drag appears to satisfy the criteria for a viable politics of resistance, one that Butler opposes to the ideality of Wittig's revolutionary lesbian body: "the normative focus for gay and lesbian practice ought to be on the subversive and parodic redeployment of power rather than on the impossible fantasy of its full-scale transcendence."[22]

But how subversive is parody? Butler's argument against unequivocal gendered identities is most powerful when it is seen as a strategic response to the social emphasis on such identities and the terror of trespassing body boundaries. As an assault on *any* coherent identity, it forecloses the possibility of a gay or lesbian specificity (erasing along the way the very discipline—gay and lesbian studies—within which the assault is made): resistance to the heterosexual matrix is reduced to more or less naughty imitations of that matrix. At its worst, the emphasis on parody in *Gender Trouble* has the effect of exaggerating the subversive potential of merely inane behavior. Butler finds that when the gay owners of a neighborhood restaurant, having gone on vacation, put out a sign reading "She's overworked and needs a rest," they are multiplying "possible sites of application" of the feminine, revealing "the arbitrary relation between the signifier and the signified" and destabilizing and mobilizing the sign.[23] Heavy stuff for some silly and familiar campiness. Furthermore, the politics of parody necessarily underplays the elements of longing and veneration in parodistic displays. The leather queen and D. A. Miller's "gay male macho body" are parodistic somewhat at their own expense: if their effect is to parody that which they worship, it is, in the first case, because the tough gay in leather *is* a queen (an involuntary parody of the "real thing," which he worships) and, in the second case, because erotic desire *must* complicate the display of muscles with a message of fuckability.

Then, too, the parodistic intentions of the down-and-out drag queens documented in Jennie Livingston's documentary film on Harlem drag balls, *Paris Is Burning,* were all in the minds of the middle-class academic analysts. The drag queens certainly resignified the dominant culture, but in ways that could only fortify that culture's dominance. The loving and loyal "families" they constituted could, I suppose, be thought of as an implicit critique of the frequent lack of love and loyalty in the heterosexually institutionalized family, but they remain tributes to the heterosexual ideal of the family itself. And even that critique was nothing more than the incidental side effect of what was meant to be a temporary holding position. The point for the drag queens is to get out of the drag family and become a success in the real (straight) fashion and entertainment world (as Willi Ninja did); for those who don't make that move, destitution and even death (as in the case of Venus Xtravaganza) can be counted on to break up the familial intimacies. The resignifying of heterosexual power in *Paris Is Burning* is really a tribute to that power. It shows how effectively American society can neutralize its margins: in their pathetically minute attention to the styles of a power from which they have been permanently excluded, the oppressed perform nothing more subversive than their own submission to being brainwashed, safely sequestered, and, if necessary, readied for annihilation.

Paris Is Burning reminds us that drag is not always fun and games or the fashion statement of those middle-class gay men who wear skirts out to dinner. The historical and ideological critique of identity surely deserves to inspire more than a taste for crossdressing. In all fairness to Butler, I should say that there has been less emphasis on parody in her recent work than in *Gender Trouble*. She has pulled back from the implication in that book (variously applauded and assailed by her readers) that we can perform ourselves out of gender. "For sexuality," she now argues, "cannot be summarily made or unmade."[24] Rejecting a "voluntarist" account of gender, she writes: "The misapprehension about gender performativity is this: that gender is a choice, or that gender is a role, or that gender is a construction that one puts on, as one puts on clothes in the morning, that there is a 'one' who is prior to this gender, a one who goes to the wardrobe of gender and decides with deliberation which gender it will be today."[25] This misapprehension sounds like a somewhat exasperated parody of *Gender Trouble,* which is understandable given the enthusiastic simplifications of that difficult and frequently abstract work by anti-identitarian activists.

It is nonetheless significant that Butler now emphasizes the constraints on performativity. *Paris Is Burning,* for example, "calls into question whether parodying the dominant norms is enough to displace them; indeed, whether the denaturalization of gender cannot be the very vehicle for a reconsolidation of hegemonic norms." Drag is now, "at best," "a site of a certain ambivalence," although it remains "subversive to the extent that it reflects on the imitative structure by which hegemonic gender is itself produced and disputes heterosexuality's claim on naturalness and originality."[26] The appropriation of hegemonic norms partly subverts them and partly reidealizes them.

These sensible qualifications, however, reveal how dependent on the norms even the utopian subversiveness of *Gender Trouble* was, for the *practice* of reappropriation and attempted resignification is bound to reveal the power of the norms—a power historically fortified by the numerous agencies and networks in which it is embedded—to resist resignification. More exactly, resignification cannot destroy; it merely presents to the dominant culture spectacles of politically impotent disrespect. Is this truly subversive, and, more fundamentally, what does subversive mean? Subversion, still a central term in Butler's thinking, means first of all, according to the dictionary, overthrowing a system, but in current academic political discourse it seems to mean something much weaker than that, referring to behavior that undermines generally accepted principles. It is, in any case, extremely doubtful that resignification, or redeployment, or hyperbolic miming, will ever overthrow anything. These mimetic activities are too closely imbricated in the norms they continue. As long as the cues for subversion are provided by the objects to be subverted, reappropriation may be delayed but is inevitable: reappropriation, and reidealization. Butler rather touchingly sees in the kinship in the various "houses" to which the drag queens of *Paris Is Burning* belong a lesson for all of us who live outside the heterosexual family. Though she has said that she doesn't think of those relations as simply providing a new and better version of the family, her description of the houses—as

mothering, rearing, caring, teaching, sheltering, enabling—is pretty much a catalogue of traditional family
values:

> These men "mother" one another, "house" one another,
> "rear" one another, and the resignification of the family
> through these terms is not a vain or useless imitation,
> but the social and discursive building of community, a
> community that binds, cares, and teaches, that shelters
> and enables. This is doubtless a cultural reelaboration
> of kinship that anyone outside of the privilege of het-
> erosexual family (and those within those "privileges"
> who suffer there) needs to see, to know, and to learn from,
> a task that makes none of us who are outside of het-
> erosexual "family" into absolute outsiders to this film.
> Significantly, it is in the elaboration of kinship forged
> through a resignification of the very terms which effect
> our exclusion and abjection that such a resignification
> creates the discursive and social space for community,
> that we see an appropriation of the terms of domina-
> tion that turns them toward a more enabling future.[27]

Furthermore, the houses sustain their members "in the
face of dislocation, poverty, homelessness." But the structures that sustain those ills are in no way threatened or
subverted; here resignification is little more than a con-
solatory community of victims.

Perhaps, as I will argue in my last chapter, we should
be questioning the value of community and, even more
fundamentally, the notion of relationality itself. It would
be foolish and unjust to deny that the quality of life for
gay men and women in America has markedly im-

proved precisely because a politicized gay and lesbian community does exist. But since it is also true that the improvement has left oppressive societal structures intact, we might wish to cultivate the *anti*communitarian impulses inherent in homo-ness. I'll come back to this; for the moment, we might look more closely at the dangers of our exhilaration in being a community. If, say, there is little self-criticism within the gay and lesbian community, this is partly out of fear of the academic thought police (any criticism of gay and lesbian self-promotion is condemned as homophobic), and partly because some of us feel it is nobler to keep our annoyances to ourselves (to voice them would be to betray the common cause, to give ammunition to the enemy). Still, we are not exactly in the position of jailed and murdered dissidents under Stalin or even of those Americans pursued by the House Un-American Committee in the early 1950s. If many gays and lesbians continue to suffer in America, it is also true that we have more clout than ever before, and that it is probably less acceptable then ever before to be openly homophobic. We have enough freedom, even enough power, to stop feeling like traitors if we cease to betray our intelligence for the sake of the cause, and if—to repeat one of the least appreciated lines in "Is the Rectum a Grave?"— we admit to having told a few lies about ourselves (and others).

We have, most notably, a propensity for making statements that no one, including the person who makes them, can truly believe. There is a difference between proposing, as Wittig does, that heterosexuality be studied as a mode of thought, not merely a preference, and claiming, as Adrienne Rich has, that it is not even a preference. The biggest concession Rich makes to heterosexual women is that she sympathizes with the difficulty they have in giving up the illusion that they choose to be heterosexual: "to acknowledge that for women heterosexuality may not be a 'preference' at all but something that has had to be imposed, managed, organized, propagandized, and maintained by force is an immense step to take if you consider yourself freely and 'innately' heterosexual." Any exclusive sexual preference—more profoundly, even sexual desire for other persons—may require some explanation, but immediately before the passage just quoted Rich exempts lesbianism from any such requirement (it has unjustly "been treated as exceptional rather than intrinsic"). At the same time, the "lesbian continuum" desexualizes lesbianism by accommodating a range of "woman-identified experience" (such as "the sharing of a rich inner life, the bonding against male tyranny, the giving and receiving of practical and political support") that goes beyond mere sexual experience with another woman. Perhaps the chief political consequence of this generous definition is to make oppressed women aware of how little they have in common with gay men. More specifically, in being "like motherhood, a profoundly *female* experience," lesbianism sharply, and virtuously, distinguishes itself from the unacceptable "prevalence of anonymous sex and the justification of pederasty among male homosexuals, the pronounced ageism in male homosexual standards of sexual attractiveness, and so forth" (what else might be included in that ominous etcetera?).[28] Such statements, which are frequently read as social documentation rather than as moral prescription, obviously create a propitious atmosphere for such dictates as Sheila Jeffreys' that, in having an orgasm with a man, a woman is "eroticizing her own oppression."[29] Thus the legitimate and necessary struggle against the oppression of women has provided a good opportunity for personal revulsion to express itself as political insight and integrity.

Puritanical feminism has of course not gone unchallenged. In the same volume that reprinted Rich's "Compulsory Heterosexuality and Lesbian Existence," Amber Hollibaugh and Cherríe Moraga make a spirited argument against the "neutered" sexuality of much feminist theory, and Gayle Rubin has consistently protested against "a lesbian politic that seems ashamed of lesbian desire."[30] Furthermore, sexual puritanism is probably less influential in both feminism and gay male discourse today than it was a decade ago. (Think of all the anti-promiscuous sermonizing by gays in the early years of the AIDS epidemic. If we were dying, we had only our loose selves to blame. Even now Larry Kramer is still at it, and recent objections in the gay press to a new bathhouse in San Francisco sounded like Randy Shilts all over again.)

Yet there continues to be a denial of sex that seems to me more harmful, and more insidiously pervasive, than the transparent aversion to sex of platonic lesbianism. Since Foucault's historical critique of the categories of sex, it has become fashionable for gay and lesbian theorists to show they are no longer being brainwashed by heterosexist society into thinking of those categories as natural. Thus in his study of "the erotics of male culture in ancient Greece," David Halperin argues that "it is not immediately evident that differences in sexual preference are by their very nature more revealing about the temperament of individual human beings, more significant determinants of personal identity, than, for example, differences in dietary preference."[31] The very title of Halperin's work is provocative: *One Hundred Years of Homosexuality* refers not to the ancient period being studied but to the modern century that gave birth to the decidedly un-Greek phenomenon of "the homosexual." What interests me here is that remark on dietary preference, which we may find as surprising as Judith Butler's contention that the only "necessarily common element among lesbians" is a knowledge of how homophobia works against women.[32] Such statements are valuable for their very absurdity, as unexpected and aggressive counterattacks against the more pervasive cultural aggression that commands us, first of all, to say who we are and, second, to give our answer in the terms furnished by the question. But what's troubling is that, in rejecting the essentializing identities derived from sexual preference, they mount a resistance to homophobia in which the agent of resistance has been erased: there is no longer any homosexual subject to oppose the homophobic subject. The desirable social transgressiveness of gayness— its aptitude for contesting oppressive structures—depends not on denying a gay identity, but rather on exploring the links between a specific sexuality, psychic mobility, and a potentially radical politics.

There is much suspicion in gay studies of inquiries into the etiology of homosexuality. "It would seem to

me," Eve Kosofsky Sedgwick writes, "that gay-affirmative work does well when it aims to minimize its reli-
ance on any particular account of the origin of sexual
preference and identity in individuals."[33] Halperin is
even more categorical: "the search for a 'scientific' ae-
tiology of sexual orientation is itself a homophobic project."[34] Such suspicions are well founded: I appreciate
Sedgwick's eagerness to do away with an essentialist-
constructivist terminology developed within "essentially
gay-genocidal nexuses of thought."[35] The double bind
in the essentialist-constructivist, or nature-nurture, debate is clear. Since the very question of "how we got
that way" would in many quarters not be asked if it
were not assumed that we ended up the wrong way, the
purpose behind the question has generally been to learn
how we might best go back and right the wrong. If the
culprit is upbringing, there is psychoanalytic therapy,
and if the trouble is in our genes, there is, or soon will
be, genetic engineering to repair the abnormality and
abortions to save society from the prenatally identified
gay child. It is important to note that for such geneti-
cists as Simon LeVay (the star expert witness for the
pro-gay side in the Colorado Amendment 2 case), demonstrations of the genetic basis of sexual preference
prove that homosexuality is just as natural and unchosen
as heterosexuality. Ideally, this would put an end to
anti-gay prejudice. But it can just as easily comfort the
homophobe with the exhilarating promise of the genetic eradication of homosexuality itself.[36]

And yet, given the fact that our distaste for etiological inquiries is certainly not going to put an end to
them, and since both the genetic and the developmental

investigations have gay supporters, we might do well to consider the disadvantages of turning our backs on these inquiries. To reject them is a major step in the de-gaying process I've been criticizing. Etiological investigation narrows the notion of identity to a very specific question: how to account for same-sex sexual desire. It brings us back to something that, for reasons that bear looking into, we prefer to keep on the margins of our social visibility: the fact that when we speak of gay rights, we are speaking of rights for men whose primary erotic pleasure is taken from the bodies of other men, and for women whose primary erotic pleasure is taken from the bodies of other women. I don't think the marginalizing of this fact indicates a kind of collective *pudeur* among gay people, or even a feeling that since the fact is so obvious it's hardly worth making a point of.[37] In fact, the point is both our specificity and our strength. As I mentioned earlier, recent psychoanalytically inspired studies have emphasized the defensive and traumatic nature of the so-called normative development of desire. An exclusively heterosexual orientation in men, for example, may depend on a misogynous identification with the father and a permanent equating of femininity with castration. The male's homosexual desire, to the extent that it depends on an identification with the mother, has already detraumatized sexual difference (by internalizing it) *and* set the stage for a relation to the father in which the latter would no longer have to be marked as the Law, the agent of castration (more on this in the next chapter). Homosexual desire is less liable to be immobilized than heterosexual desire in that, structurally, it occupies several positions.

Its privileging of sameness has, as its condition of possibility, an indeterminate identity. Homosexual desire is desire for the same from the perspective of a self already identified as different from itself.

In saying this, am I encouraging essentializing definitions of desire? There is an important difference between acquiescing in an imposed identity (the homosexual as a particular case of arrested development, for example, with all the characterological consequences of that misfortune) and displaying an active curiosity about the fantasies and identifications that have helped to constitute certain sexual preferences. For those preferences do exist and, like all preferences, they involve exclusions. Gay men mainly go to bed with other men (thus excluding women) and lesbians—*pace* Wittig—do "associate, make love, live with women" (thus excluding men). The political danger of admitting something so obvious must be very great indeed; it has even led, as we have seen, to a suspicion of sexual difference itself as a heterosexist plot. Again, though, there is a difference between realizing how much "woman" is a cultural construct, and even how the definition of the biological differences between the sexes has been ideologically biased, and on the other hand recognizing that in our most intimate relations, in our demand for equal rights, in our elaborating a discipline we call gay history, we are constantly acknowledging that difference.

My argument is not that homosexuals are better than heterosexuals. Instead, it is to suggest that same-sex desire, while it excludes the other sex as its object, presupposes a desiring subject for whom the antagonism between the different and the same no longer exists. This is not to revert to the rightly discredited definition of homosexuality as a woman's soul in a man's body. That makes gay men a freakish instance of gender misassignments. They somehow received the wrong soul (or the wrong gene), and if they are therefore sexual anomalies, their sexual behavior is at least consistent since it conforms to the nature they have erroneously received. I am speaking of something different—not of a mysteriously predetermined and permanently fixed orientation, but of the inevitable, unpredictable, and variable process by which desire becomes attached to persons. How does the wish to repeat pleasurable stimulations of the body translate into, or come to constitute, intersubjectivity? If the infant's pleasures are already constituted by a relation (to the mother providing those pleasures), the connection between the autoerotic and the intersubjective, though it is constitutive of human beings from the very start, also has to be learned. We share with animals the need to repeat pleasures; what may be distinctively human is the interposition, between the need and its satisfaction, of scenarios of desire that *select* the agents of our pleasure. (Animals also choose their sexual partners, but do scenarios of desire enter into the process?) This selection is an imitation—or rather, an identification with other desiring subjects. It is not a woman's soul in a man's body that leads him to desire other men, but, within what might be called the available social field of desiring subjects, the incorporation of woman's otherness may be a major source of desiring material for male homosexuals.

In a heterosexual society, women play a major role,

at once psychic and corporeal, in teaching the gay man
how to frame and to stage his sexuality. Furthermore,
as Kaja Silverman has argued, the gay man's deployment of signifiers of the feminine may be a powerful
weapon in the defeat of those defensive maneuvers that
have defined sexual difference.[38] This goal, one might
add, is also served by the instability of the deployment.
The gay man's identification with women is countered
by an imitation of those desiring subjects with whom
we have been officially identified: other men. In a sense,
then, the very maintaining of the couples man-woman,
heterosexual-homosexual, serves to break down their
oppositional distinctions. These binary divisions help
to create the diversified desiring field across which we
can move, thus reducing sexual difference itself—at least
as far as desire is concerned—to a merely formal arrangement inviting us to transgress the very identity assigned
to us within the couple.[39]

It is not possible to be gay-affirmative, or politically
effective as gays, if gayness has no specificity. Being gay
has certain political consequences, which may lead us
into making alliances with other oppressed groups. But
in ignoring or feeling guilty about what makes us different from the others, we run the risk of blinding ourselves to how that difference can complicate and even
destroy the alliances. Some prominent African-Americans, for instance, have not hesitated to express resent-
ment at any suggestion that homosexuals' status as
victims in American society is analogous to theirs. Since
the furor over allowing, or rather acknowledging, gays
in the military reminded many people of the resistance

to racial integration in the armed forces a half-century ago, there has been ample opportunity both to blur and to exaggerate the disparity. Although blacks are probably a more powerful political constituency in America today than gays, and although there are ways in which homosexuals, unlike an underprivileged racial minority, represent a threat to American society unresponsive to genuine social and economic reform, it is still true that a middle-class white gay man can hardly claim to know the sort of oppression suffered by black men and women and, even more pointedly, an economically disadvantaged black gay man or woman. As Henry Louis Gates Jr. has pointed out, "measured by their position in society, gays on the average seem privileged relative to blacks; measured by the acceptance of hostile attitudes toward them, gays are worse off than blacks."[40]

In any case, given the numerous and often contradictory differences at work here, if it is futile to argue about degrees of victimization, it is also absurd to claim that a privileged white gay male (like me) can speak for gay or straight African-Americans. We may, as decent human beings, choose to speak *with* them (and to accept Gloria Anzaldúa's invitation to meet other cultures "halfway"[41]), but we should expect occasional (only occasional if we're lucky) manifestations of black homophobia and gay racism. At the same time, we should also remember that—however privileged we are as individuals—we belong to a minority despised not only by the powerful but also, often with greater vehemence and even more self-righteously, by the most luckless racial and economic victims in every part of the world.

To remember that may help gay men to stop apologizing for not belonging to a racial minority (if we are white) or to an economically underprivileged class (if we are well off). Gay pride often seems identical to gay shame. When we are scolded for speaking like advantaged white males, we beg to be instructed by those demonstrably more oppressed than we are. Even more remarkably, we have even been heard to apologize for not being women. The relation of gay men to feminism is bound to be more problematic than anyone wants to admit. I have argued against a tendency among gay activists to ignore the connections between political sympathies and sexual fantasies. There can be, I suggested, a continuity between a sexual preference for rough and uniformed trade, a sentimentalizing of the armed forces, and right-wing politics.[42] Such continuities can be particularly troublesome in the relation of gay men to women. Our feminist sympathies (perhaps nourished, as Silverman claims, by our desiring from the same "position" as women) can't help being complicated by an inevitable narcisstic investment in the objects of our desire. If the genealogy of desire is always also a history of the subject's identifications, and if this means that the desire to have is never entirely distinct from the desire to be, the boundaries between having and being are bound to be more blurred in same-gender desire than in heterosexual desire. The former *begins* with a recognition of sameness; the latter includes (and struggles to overcome) the memory of a traumatic encounter with difference. In his desires, the gay man always runs the risk of identifying with culturally dominant images of misogynist maleness. For the sexual drives of gay men do, after all, extend beyond the rather narrow circle of other politically correct gay men. A more or less secret sympathy with heterosexual male misogyny carries with it the narcissistically gratifying reward of confirming our membership in (and not simply our erotic appetite for) the privileged male society.

I certainly don't mean that political alignments can be wholly accounted for by fantasy identifications. To forestall any such misunderstanding, I hasten to say that you can be turned on by sailors without being a right-wing militarist. Our fantasy investments are often countered by more consciously and more rationally elaborated modes of reaching out to others, such as liking or admiring people we don't desire. In that tension lies an important moral dimension of our political engagement. But to be aware of the tension means being aware of both sets of determining factors, especially of those identifications and erotic interests it is not always gratifying to acknowledge. The cultural constraints under which we operate include not only visible political structures but also the fantasmatic processes by which we eroticize the real. Even if we are straight or gay at birth, we still have to learn to desire particular men and women, and not to desire others; the *economy* of our sexual drives is a cultural achievement. Perhaps nowhere are we manipulated more effectively and more insidiously than in our most personal choices or tastes in the objects of our desires. Those choices have cultural origins and political consequences. To understand what might be called the line of constraint running from one to the other is itself a political imperative.

The fantasy underpinnings of gay men's feminism become particularly fragile when our feminist allies are lesbians. From the perspective of identification theory, the gay and lesbian community, which does exist, is something of a miracle. As lesbians and gay men have drawn closer to one another, the old dream of friendship between men and women seems finally to have become a viable social achievement—as if, ironically, sadly, it depended on a certain absence of interest, as if, to put it crudely, coming together depended precisely on not coming together. The union, as might be expected, has not been untroubled. With heterosexual women we at least share their desires, just as straight men, while ignorant of *how* a lesbian desires, turn in their desires toward many of the same images to which a woman loving women would be drawn. It is hardly surprising that "fantasy" has become a politically incorrect word. If we think of how remote lesbian desiring fantasies are, by definition, from gay male desiring fantasies, and if we acknowledge the influence of erotic investments on political choices, then the very notion of fantasy could easily seem like a heterosexist scheme to sow discord in the gay-lesbian community. Men loving men, women loving women: the separation between the sexes could hardly be more radical. Still, across that chasm, new kinds of bridges have been invented, not only of disinterested friendship but also, in some cases, of an unpressured and, so to speak, new genre of heterosexual desire (of a gay man for a woman he can *count on* not to desire him, of a lesbian for a man she can *count on* not to desire her).[43]

Even if we leave aside failed psychic identifications,

there is of course a social chasm separating gay men from lesbians. The most solid foundation for our alliance is oppression: discrimination as a result of same-gender sexual preference. Yet lesbians are an oppressed group sexually invested in an oppressed group. Gay men are an oppressed group not only sexually drawn to the power-holding sex but also belonging to it themselves. No wonder lesbians (especially during the early years of gay liberation) have been so suspicious of the gay men with whom they are presumably united in a common cause. We are in fact pariahs among minorities and oppressed groups. Feminists speak with distaste of our promiscuous male sexuality; African-Americans accuse us of neglecting the crucial issues of class and race for such luxuries as "gay identity." As white middle-class gay men, we are too much like our oppressors, which means that we can never be sufficiently oppressed. And so, without renouncing our privileges, we keep on apologizing for them. We are mortified if we are white and prosperous; and insofar as the "male 'I' has enjoyed something of a psychic and cultural monopoly on subjectivity that needs to be dissolved," we will seek to be born again, this time engendered, as a recent book puts it, by feminism, in the anxious hope of deconstructing our repellently renascent male selves.[44]

Without questioning the good faith or the intelligence of those who make such announcements of self-erasure, we should view them with suspicion. Male homosexuality has always manifested itself socially as a highly specific blend of conformism and transgression. For an impoverished African-American, to conform is to embrace the racial and economic injustices

from which he or she suffers; for a woman, to conform
is to accept a heterosexist definition of female identity;
for most gay men, to conform is to pick up the perqui-
sites waiting for them as men. As the debate about gays
in the military has confirmed, society is willing to give
a gay man equal opportunity if he makes his gayness
invisible. This is hardly the contract it has with racial
minorities, with the poor, or with women. The social
agenda of gay men can make such conformism seem
relatively painless. For we want something which is
unique among oppressed groups: the right to have the
sex we want without being punished for it. It is demeaning to agree to hide who we are; it is commend-
able to insist, as we have begun to do, that we reject
the terms of our social contract. It is nonetheless a significant fact of the social being of a very large number
of gay white males that we have always had the option
of power and privilege. Nothing a woman agrees to do
for the dominant culture will ever give her all the privileges intrinsic to maleness; nothing Clarence Thomas
agrees to do will ever make him completely white. The
pressures of the double lives gay people have been forced
to lead can be enormous, but even those pressures are
something of a luxury. If we can live with them, and if
we don't get caught (and those "ifs" should not be mini-
mized), the advantages are very great indeed: potentially unlimited vistas of social opportunity and all the
sex we want, if necessary, on the sly.

Things have changed. No more hiding, no more guilty
transgressive sex. But the habit of invisibility has been
so strong that even in coming out we have managed to
hide ourselves. So, once again, we melt in—either into

those other groups whose oppressed state we yearn to
share or into mainstream America. The former assimilation may be more politically meritorious than the
latter, but to glide from one to the other is easy, especially if both are grounded in the same pursuit of invisibility. A pertinent question might be: what has straight
America seen in our new presence? We want to be
recognized, but not as homosexuals (the essentialist
identity). It is doubtful that we will be mistaken for
other oppressed groups by the dominant culture (which
is, for obvious reasons, concerned with questions of
identity); we may, however, easily be mistaken for the
dominant culture. The mistake can be forgiven, since
we ourselves like to place gayness at the center not only
of American society but also of western civilization. In
Epistemology of the Closet, Eve Kosofsky Sedgwick
goes so far as to propose that

> many of the major nodes of thought and knowledge in
> twentieth-century Western culture as a whole are struc-
> tured—indeed, fractured—by a chronic, now endemic
> crisis of homo-heterosexual definition, indicatively male,
> dating from the end of the nineteenth century . . . An
> understanding of virtually any aspect of modern West-
> ern culture must be, not merely incomplete, but dam-
> aged in its central substance to the degree that it does
> not incorporate a critical analysis of modern homo-het-
> erosexual definition.[45]

Sedgwick argues her claim with great eloquence, but it
is probably less useful to determine how right she is
than to note how breathtaking the claim itself is. It rips
us right out of our marginal sexual skins and relocates

us, distinguished and disincarnate, at the very heart of epistemological endeavor, at the root of the western pursuit of knowledge. Lee Edelman has undertaken a fascinating but analogously de-gaying enterprise in his attempt to unpack "representations of gay sexuality in terms of the anxieties condensed therein about the logic of representation as such." For Edelman, "the signifier 'gay' comes to name the unknowability of sexuality as such, the unknowability that *is* sexuality as such." Homosexuality is "the reified figure of the unknowable within the field of 'sexuality.'" The value of "acts of gay self-nomination" is thus exactly equivalent to their negativizing, self-destructing potential: such acts "maintain their disruptive capacity by refusing to offer any determinate truth about the nature or management of 'gay' sexuality."[46]

To move to an entirely different register, Tony Kushner's *Angels in America* has analogous ambitions. For Kushner, to be gay in the 1980s was to be a metaphor not only for Reagan's America but for the entire history of America, a country in which there are "no gods . . . no ghosts and spirits . . . no angels . . . no spiritual past, no racial past, there's only the political."[47] The enormous success of this muddled and pretentious play is a sign, if we need still another one, of how ready and anxious America is to see and hear about gays—provided we reassure America how familiar, how morally sincere, and, particularly in the case of Kushner's work, how innocuously full of significance we can be.

By both applauding such reductions and assimilations, and claiming at the same time that we are different without being willing to define that difference, we merely position ourselves for reproaches and reprisals from all those groups bound to discover eventually what separates us from them. "Men in feminism," for example, is bound to lead to angry complaints about "feminism without women." That is the title of a book by Tania Modleski, who compares the relation between feminism and some of its contemporary male theorists to that of the mother and the male child in Gille Deleuze's notion of masochism: "the male child allies himself with the mother against the law of the father, which it is the function of the mother to beat out of the son." For these theorists, Modleski argues, "feminism itself has come to occupy the position of the mother who is identified with the law." But this alliance "is doomed to failure, from a feminist point of view, unless the father is frankly confronted and the entire dialectic of abjection and the law worked through; otherwise, as Deleuze's analysis confirms, the father will always remain in force as the major, if hidden, point of reference—and he may in fact be expected at any time to emerge from hiding with a vengeance."[48] Male feminism thus risks remaining an affair (yet another one) strictly between men, attesting once more to the extraordinary difficulty men have—not in speaking *for* women or *through* women to each other, but in *addressing* women.

The possibility of a constitutive inability in maleness (both heterosexual and homosexual) to address women is elided by the more comforting project of grouping politically against a common enemy (who, still firmly in power, hardly bothers to answer the charge). Fantasmatic complicities are denied through a deceptively self-

immolating participation in the struggle against the evil
Law of an evil patriarchy, thus making it even more
difficult to struggle against those complicities, that is,
against men's massive and complex investment in the
Law. Furthermore, gay male sexuality is as prone as
any other mode of sexual expression to contradictions
not entirely reducible to bad social arrangements. By
attributing the inevitable suffering and struggle for power
between intimately related individuals to the nefarious
influence of patriarchal culture, gay and lesbian activists have found a convenient if rather mean-spirited way
of denying human distress. To admit that being a gay
man or a lesbian involves a certain sexual specificity,
and even to go so far as to wonder about the psychic
structures and origins of that specificity, might impli-
cate us in that distress by forcing us to see the gay take
on what is politically unfixable in the human.

Our de-gaying resources seem limitless. Most recently,
we have decided to be queer rather than gay. The history of *gay* is too bound up with efforts to define a
homosexual identity. But *queer* has a double advantage: it repeats, with pride, a pejorative straight word
for homosexual even as it unloads the term's homosexual referent. For oppressed groups to accept the queer
label is to identify themselves as being actively at odds
with a male-dominated, white, capitalistic, heterosexist
culture. Gay becomes one aspect in Michael Warner's
"resistance to regimes of the normal." This generous
definition puts all resisters in the same queer bag—a
universalizing move I appreciate but that fails to spec-
ify the sexual distinctiveness of the resistance. I find this

particularly unfortunate since queer theorists protest, albeit ambiguously, against the exclusion of the sexual from the political. Queerness would seem to be, in large part, an emphasis on the inextricability of the sexual and the political, although its theorists often understand the connection in a peculiarly nonsexual way.[49] Steven Seidman, in his impressive contribution to Warner's collection of essays in queer theory, details the connection between sexuality and social positioning:

> Sexual orientational status positions the self in the social periphery or the social center; it places the self in a determinate relation to institutional resources, social opportunities, legal protections and social privileges; it places the self in a relation to a range of forms of social control, from violence to ridicule. Locating identity in a multidimensional social space features its macrosocial significance; we are compelled to relate the politics of representation to institutional dynamics.[50]

This lays the ground for valuable work, work that risks remaining in fundamental agreement, however, with the society it would contest on the value of sociality itself as that society has already defined it. To what extent does queer theory do more than add new categories, and occasionally new discursive styles, to classical leftist analysis? Warner argues that "because the logic of the sexual order is so deeply embedded by now in an indescribably wide range of social institutions, and is embedded in the most standard accounts of the world, queer struggles aim not just at toleration or equal status but at challenging those institutions and accounts."[51] But unless we define how the sexual specificity of being queer (a specificity perhaps common to the myriad ways of being queer and the myriad conditions in which one is queer) gives queers a special aptitude for making that challenge, we are likely to come up with a remarkably familiar, and merely liberal, version of it.

In a brilliant essay on Thoreau, Warner does document the political productivity of a particular sexuality. He traces the link between anality in Thoreau and the "paradigmatically liberal problems of self-possession and mutuality," thus giving a persuasive illustration of how "political systems are always inhabited by the body."[52] But in *Fear of a Queer Planet*, his formulation of a queer political challenge is itself paradigmatically liberal: "Being queer . . . means being able, more or less articulately, to challenge the common understanding of what gender difference means, or what the state is for, or what 'health' entails, or what would define fairness, or what a good relation to the planet's environment would be." It seems peculiarly dismissive of the majority of human beings to suggest that you have to be queer to understand what fairness is or what health entails—unless of course queer is stripped of its sexual mark and is simply a *consequence* of an understanding of fairness and health. If queerness means more than simply taking sexuality into account in our political analyses, if it means that modalities of desire are not only effects of social operations but are at the core of our very imagination of the social and political, then something has to be said about how erotic desire for the same might revolutionize our understanding of how the human subject is, or might be, socially implicated.

Seidman's program is even more reminiscent of straight-inflected liberal politics (as well as of the straight seriousness of Marxist-inspired writing). Once we recognize that identity is only a social positioning, we can effectively "address specific conflicts" and engage in appropriate politics: "local struggles for participatory democracy, distributive social justice, lifestyle choice, or reconfiguring knowledges." "Local" and "pragmatic" are key words in Seidman's political aims. Postmodern culture rightly abandons "millennial vision" and "anticipation of the 'end of domination' or self realization"; its analyses "do not shy away from spelling out a vision of a better society in terms resonant to policy makers and activists." This rather sad if realistic modesty leads to a preference for "social sketches, framed in a more narrative rather than analytic mode." Localized stories can both situate particular points of identitarian pressure *and,* aware of those constraints, wrest at least some control, in Cindy Patton's terms, over the discourses of identity construction. Thus we would strategically participate in those "rhetorical closures" that constitute identities, creating, I suppose, something like micro-dissonances, micropoints of resistance that performatively compete with the hegemonic "grammar of identity construction."[53]

Somewhat differently, the antics of Queer Nation have combined the local with the global. Now it is a question of crossing borders, of occupying normal spaces in order "to dismantle the standardizing apparatus that organizes all manner of sexual practice into 'facts' of sexual *identity.*" As Lauren Berlant and Elizabeth Freeman write, Queer Nation disrupts "the semiotic boundaries between gay and straight. The group's parodies and reconstructions of mainstream ads inflect products with a sexuality and promote homosexuality as a product: they lay bare the queerness of the commodities that straight culture makes and buys, either translating it from its hidden form in the original, or revealing and ameliorating its calculated erasure." These tactics are aggressive but fundamentally good-natured. Citizenship is "voluntary and consensual, democratic and universalist." In short, Queer Nation complicates and enriches the social with its campy replications of given forms of the social. It does not put into question sociality itself. To do *that* may be the most radical political potential of queerness. For this reason I was particularly intrigued by the final pages of Berlant's and Freeman's essay, where they contrast the essential geniality of Queer Nation with a "negation of their own audience" that they find characteristic of certain parts of zine culture. "Application for citizenship in the Bitch Nation, for example, repudiates the promise of community in common readership, the privileges of a common language, the safety of counteridentity."[54] My discussions of Gide and Genet should make clear why I think it important to consider further the value of these repudiations.

Warner notes that "the notion of a community has remained problematic if only because nearly every lesbian or gay remembers being such before entering a collectively identified space, because much of lesbian and gay history has to do with noncommunity, and because dispersal rather than localization continues to be definitive of queer self-understanding." Drawing on Hannah Arendt's description of modern social conform-ity, where rulebreakers are deemed abnormal, Warner concludes that queers are objecting to "the cultural phenomenon of societalization." But the value of this suggestion is somewhat lessened by reducing protest to a response to "the normalizing methodologies of modern social knowledge."[55] There is a more radical possibility: *homo-ness itself necessitates a massive redefining of relationality.* More fundamental than a resistance to normalizing methodologies is a potentially revolutionary inaptitude—perhaps inherent in gay desire—for sociality as it is known.

I'm not proposing a return to immobilizing definitions of identity. To say that there is a gay specificity doesn't commit us to the notion of a homosexual essence. Indeed, we may discover that this particularity, in its indeterminateness and mobility, is not at all compatible with essentializing definitions. In evading questions of specificity, even of identity and etiology, we are setting ourselves up for that inevitable judgment day when we will be found guilty of our gayness and will begin again, uselessly, to apologize for it. But if the kind of investigation I have in mind brings us up against some politically unpleasant facts, we may discover, within the very ambiguities of being gay, a path of resistance far more threatening to dominant social orders than vestimentary blurrings of sexual difference and possibly subversive separations of sex from gender. There are some glorious precedents for thinking of homosexuality as truly disruptive—as a *force* not limited to the modest goals of tolerance for diverse lifestyles, but in fact mandating the politically unacceptable and politically indispensable choice of an outlaw existence.

3

The Gay Daddy

"I think that what most bothers those who are not gay about gayness is the gay life-style, not sex acts themselves . . . It is the prospect that gays will create as yet unforeseen kinds of relationships that many people cannot tolerate."[1] The desexualizing of homophobia implicit in this quote from an interview Michel Foucault gave to the American magazine *Salmagundi* was by no means incidental to the mood of a single conversation. In an interview that appeared in 1988 in the French gay publication *Mec,* Foucault said: "People can tolerate two homosexuals they see leaving together, but if the next day they're smiling, holding hands and tenderly embracing one another, then they can't be forgiven. It is not the departure for pleasure that is intolerable, it is waking up happy."[2] For someone who has proposed—

as I have in "Is the Rectum a Grave?"—that homophobia may be the vicious expression of a more or less hidden
fantasy of males participating, principally through anal
sex, in what is presumed to be the terrifying phenomenon of female sexuality, Foucault's argument naturally,
or perversely, has a strong appeal. The intolerance of
gayness, far from being the displaced expression of
the anxieties that nourish misogyny, would be nothing
more—by which of course Foucault meant nothing less—
than a political anxiety about the subversive, revolutionary social rearrangements that gays may be trying
out. Indeed, in this scenario there may be no fantasies—in the psychoanalytic sense—on either side, and
if there are, they are insignificant in understanding the
threat of gayness. Our culture's sense of security, Foucault goes on to suggest in the *Mec* interview, depends
on its being able to interpret. What I may have taken
as an interpretive terror of homosexual sex is nothing
more than a screen—the exciting indulgence of scary
fantasies that masks a more profound anxiety about a
threat to the way people are expected to relate to one
another, which is not too different from saying the way
power is positioned and exercised in our society.

There may be nothing to say about those gays holding hands after a night of erotic play. Don't, Foucault
warns us, read *their* tenderness as the exhausted after-
math of cocksucking that would "really" be a disguised
devouring of the mother's breast, or a fucking that
would "really" be the heterosexual repossession of a
lost phallic woman, or a being fucked that would "really" be the obsessively controlled reenactment of the
mother's castration by the father in the primal scene.

No, those homosexuals gaily embracing as they go to breakfast in the Castro or somewhere off Christopher Street are blankly, superficially, radically, threateningly happy. "There is," Foucault says, "no anxiety, there is no fantasy behind happiness," and with no fantasies to fantasize about, the silenced interpreter becomes the intolerant homophobe. In French: "Il n'y a pas d'angoisse, il n'y a pas de fantasme derrière le bonheur, aussi on ne tolère plus."[3]

Although nearly everything I have ever thought or written about sexuality is at odds with that reading of homophobic intolerance, I have begun to think of it as quite appealing, nearly irresistible. If I add "nearly" it is partly because, having always longed to be one of those happy gays myself, I can't help wondering what the pleasures were that led to this enviable absence of any interpretive aftertaste in the men Foucault probably did see, less frequently, I would guess, in Paris than around Castro Street where he lived when, during the glorious pre-AIDS years of the late 1970s, he was a visiting professor at Berkeley. Foucault says almost nothing about those pleasures in the interviews I refer to, although he did speak elsewhere at some length, and with enthusiasm, of gay sadomasochistic sex. In a discussion printed in 1984 in the *Advocate,* Foucault praised S/M practitioners as "inventing new possibilities of pleasure with strange parts of their bodies." He called S/M "a creative enterprise, which has as one of its main features what I call the desexualization of pleasure." In a complaint that clearly echoes the call, at the end of the first volume of his *History of Sexuality,* for "a different economy of bodies and pleasures," Foucault adds: "The idea that bodily pleasure should always come from sexual pleasure, and the idea that sexual pleasure is the root of *all* our possible pleasure—I think *that's* something quite wrong."[4]

So there is much more to erotic pleasure than sex (by which I take Foucault to mean the conventional association of pleasure with genital stimulation), and, perhaps most interestingly, once we desexualize the erotic we may also be moving to save it from interpretation. It is as if desexualized pleasures were pleasures without fantasy, almost pleasure uncomplicated by desire, and this displacement of pleasure from the genitals to what Foucault somewhat enigmatically refers to as "strange parts of our body, in very unusual situations" will, I presume, beneficently frustrate all those interpretive efforts based on the idea that pleasure is only sexual. I'll return to this notion of a desexualized, defantasized body and, in particular, to what such an idea implies for thinking about the connection between the way we take our pleasure and the way we exercise power. For the moment, I want to return to those two happy men and, without wishing to explain or interpret their happiness, at least conjecture about how they spent the night. Given what Foucault says about S/M, it is not at all improbable that a few moments before Foucault's observer passed them, they checked out of the much-lamented Slot, an S/M bathhouse in San Francisco, now closed, where one of the two—and roles may have been switched during the night—whipped, fistfucked, verbally abused, and singed the nipples of the other. Far from making such a suggestion in order to question the unreadability of their post-torture tenderness, I want instead to propose—as I think Foucault meant to—that the intolerable promise of "unforseen kinds of relationships" which many people see in gay lifestyles cannot be dissociated from an authentically new organization of the body's pleasures; and to suggest that such a program may necessarily involve some radical, perhaps even dangerous, experimentation with modes of what used to be called making love.

No one was more alert than Foucault to the connections between how we organize our pleasures with one other person and the larger forms of social organization. It is the original thesis of his *History* that power in our societies functions primarily not by repressing spontaneous sexual drives but by producing multiple sexualities, and that through the classification, distribution, and moral rating of those sexualities the individuals practicing them can be approved, treated, marginalized, sequestered, disciplined, or normalized. The most effective resistance to this disciplinary productivity should, Foucault suggests, take the form not of a struggle against prohibition, but rather of a kind of counter-productivity. It is not a question of lifting the barriers to seething repressed drives, but of consciously, deliberately playing on the surfaces of our bodies with forms or intensities of pleasure not covered, so to speak, by the disciplinary classifications that have until now taught us what sex is.

What strikes me as most interesting about this argument is a connection that Foucault appears to deny in the *Salmagundi* interview when he says that it is not sex acts themselves that are most troubling to nongays, but the gay lifestyle, those "as yet unforseen kinds of relationships." There is a neat tactical displacement of emphasis in this sentence: 'Don't think,' Foucault is saying to nongays, 'that you're going to get off with a Freudian reduction of your homophobia to personal anxieties; what you're really afraid of is the threat to your privileges in the gay escape from relationships you created in order to protect that power.' But Foucault everywhere implies that a new lifestyle, new kinds of relationships, are indissociable from new sex acts—or, in his preferred terms, from a new economy of bodily pleasure. In the same interview in which he appears to dissociate sex acts from lifestyles, he notes that most homosexuals today—like the ancient Greeks—feel that "being the passive partner in a love relationship" is "in some way demeaning," and he goes on to say that "S/M has actually helped to alleviate this problem somewhat."[5] S/M, he is suggesting—partly due to the frequent reversibility of roles, partly as a result of the demonstration S/M is said to provide of the power of bottoms, or presumed slaves—has helped to empower a position traditionally associated with female sexuality.

To empower the disenfranchised partner is, however, not at all the same thing as eliminating struggles for power in erotic negotiations. Foucault obviously thought we would be better off if we could finally shed our compulsion to know and to tell the "truth" of desire, but he never claimed that a new economy of the body, or unforseen relationships, would not continue to be, in perhaps unforseen ways, exercises of power. Indeed, given the notion of power in the *History* as being everywhere, as "produced from one moment to the next, at every point, or rather in every relation from one point to another,"[6] it is extremely difficult to imagine how we might even move in the world—never mind how we might make love—without both engaging in some mildly or wildly coercive acts and producing frictions that inevitably block those coercive moves. Indeed, Foucault's thought is all the more appealing, to me, in that his utopian visions never include the pastoral promise—so fashionable in utopian vision in recent years—of predominantly caring and nurturing human intimacies. There are of course those two hauntingly happy and tender men, but given Foucault's unambiguous endorsement of S/M, one question we could investigate is the relation, if any, between a happiness unburdened by fantasies ominously lurking just behind it and, say, the consensual brutalization of bodies. Though it would be absurd to argue that sadomasochism is the royal road to an economy of still unprogrammed pleasures, S/M raises, however crudely, important questions about the relation between pleasure and the exercise of power, and invites (in spite of itself) a psychoanalytic study of the defeat, or at least the modulation, of power by the very pleasure inherent in its exercise.

This radical potential in S/M has been obscured by political claims from which, interestingly, Foucault kept a certain distance. It is frequently maintained that S/M both exposes the mechanisms of power in society and provides a cathartic release from the tensions inherent in social distributions of power. "In the sadomasochistic world," write two sympathetic sociologists, "many of the conventional niceties, which normally obscure motives and interests, are stripped away."[7] Enthusiastic practitioners echo the related themes of catharsis and exposure. Geoff Mains, for example, says that "men fraught with the tensions of social and economic striving seek contrast and relief through a relinquishing of power." "Leather," apparently the board chairman's ideal therapy, "can relieve stress."[8] It is a therapeutic bringing to the surface of what Robert Hopcke calls "the darker side of men's experience."[9] Far from contesting conventional psychological wisdom about individual unhappiness and social maladjustment, S/M offers the benefits of therapy at no financial cost, and with an erotic thrill to boot: in the words of Mark Thompson, "long-held feelings of inferiority or low self-esteem, grief and loss, familial rejection and abandonment, come to surface during S/M ritual."[10] Free association is an expensive bore; with the whip, *jouir* becomes identical to *durcharbeiten*.

Politically, the S/M'er says to society: this is the way you really are. Mains approvingly quotes Ian Young: "People [into S/M] have an opportunity to be more aware of the elements of dominance and submission in all relationships."[11] And Thompson claims: "In our audacious explicating of society's roles and violent tensions, leatherfolk mirror the deadly game that a culture dishonest with itself plays."[12] This mirroring is invariably presented as a way of contesting what is mirrored. "While the dynamics of S/M may reinforce the categorization of sex and sex roles," Young writes, "I think it is more likely to break them down."[13] As Pat Califia, one of the most intelligent writers on S/M, says: "In an S/M context, the uniforms and roles and dialogue become a parody of authority, a challenge to it, a recognition of its secret sexual nature."[14] Somehow recognition gets identified with a political challenge. To strip away "conventional niceties," to become "more aware" of inequalities of power in all relationships, to "explicate" violent social tensions, to "recognize" the "secret sexual nature" of authority: does any of this suggest much more than a nonhypocritical acceptance of power as it is already structured?

If there is some subversive potential in the reversibility of roles in S/M, a reversibility that puts into question assumptions about power inhering "naturally" in one sex or one race, S/M sympathizers have an extremely respectful attitude toward the dominance-submission dichotomy itself. Sometimes it seems that if anything in society is being challenged, it is not the networks of power and authority, but the exclusion of gays from those networks. Michael Bronski calls "the explosion of private sexual fantasy into public view . . . a powerful political statement," but it turns out that the content of that statement is a grab for power: "to consciously present oneself as a (homo)sexual being [and 'this is particularly true of the S/M leather scene'] is to grapple with and grab power for oneself."[15] If that's what you're after, then there's no reason to question the categories that define power. Most significantly, at least in gay male S/M, conventional masculinity is worshipped. While the oxymoronic phenomenon of the leather queen is often seen as attacking straight ideas of extreme masculinity, it actually expands the notion of machismo. S/M, Hopcke writes, is an "unadulterated reclamation of masculinity" on the part of those who have been excluded from that worthy ideal: gay men. The ideal itself is evident in Hopcke's luridly glamorous evocation of the (capitalized) Masculine which, once we've claimed it as ours, somehow helps us to deliver a mortal blow to the culture that invented it: "In S/M and the powerful initiation into archetypal masculinity that it represents, gay men have found a way to reclaim their primal connection to the rawness and power of the Masculine, to give a patriarchal, heterosexist society a stinging slap in the face by calling upon the masculine power of men's connection to men to break the boxes of immaturity and effeminacy into which we as gay men have been put."[16]

If the alternative to this aping of the dominant culture's ideal of dominance is not the renunciation of power itself, the question is whether we can imagine relations of power structured differently. The reversibility of roles in S/M does allow everyone to get his or her moment in the exalted position of Masculinity (and, if everyone can be a bottom, no one owns the top or dominant position), but this can be a relatively mild challenge to social hierarchies of power. Everyone gets a chance to put his or her boot in someone else's face— but why not question the value of putting on boots for that purpose in the first place? Yes, in S/M roles are reversible; yes, in S/M enslavement is consensual; yes, as Califia puts it, S/M is "power unconnected to privilege."[17] But this doesn't mean that privilege is contested; rather, you get to enjoy its prerogatives even if you're not one of the privileged. A woman gets to treat a man, or another woman, with the same brutal authority a man has exercised over her; a black man can savor the humiliation of his white trick, thus sharing the pleasure enjoyed by whites in more acceptable social contexts. Furthermore, socially sanctioned positions of power are fortified by the covert and always temporary changes of position offered by an underground culture. The transformation of the brutal, all-powerful corporate executive (by day) into the whimpering, panty-clad servant of a pitiless dominatrix (by night) is nothing more than a comparatively invigorating release of tension. The concession to a secret and potentially enervating need to shed the master's exhausting responsibilities and to enjoy briefly the irresponsibility of total powerlessness allows for a comfortable return to a position of mastery and oppression the morning after, when all that "other side" has been, at least for a time, whipped out of the executive's system.

These truths are dressed up by defenders of S/M with a lot of talk about how loving the S/M community is. Unlike nasty patriarchal society, this community only inflicts torture on people who say they want to be tortured. And the victim is always in control: he or she can stop the scene at will, unlike the victims of society's self-righteous wars. This difference is of course important. The practice of S/M depends on a mutual respect generally absent from the relations between the powerful and the weak, underprivileged, or enslaved in society. S/M is nonetheless profoundly conservative in that its imagination of pleasure is almost entirely defined by the dominant culture to which it thinks of itself as giving "a stinging slap in the face." It is true that those who exercise power generally don't admit to the excitement they derive from such exercises. To recognize this excitement may challenge the hypocrisy of authority, but it certainly doesn't challenge authority itself. On the contrary: it reveals the unshakable foundation on which power is built. Its exercise, S/M'ers never stop telling us, is thrilling, and it can be just as thrilling for the victim as for the victimizer.

No wonder Foucault, in an interview called "Sade, Sergeant of Sex," insisted that Eros was absent from Nazism (or was at most only "accidental" to it).[18] I suspect he knew that it was very much present, but he had good reason to insist on its absence. He was careful to distinguish the master-slave relation in S/M from oppressive social structures of domination. S/M, he said, is not "a reproduction, within the erotic relationship, of the structure of power. It is an acting out of power structures by a strategic game that is able to give sexual pleasure or bodily pleasure."[19] But what is the game without the power structure that constitutes its strategies? What S/M does not reproduce is the intentionality supporting the structures in society—for example, what Foucault calls "the disgusting petit-bourgeois dream of a kind of racial correctness underlying the Nazi dream."[20] True enough, but the polarized structure of master and slave, of dominance and submission, is the same in Nazism and in S/M, and that structure—not the dream of racial "purity" or the strictly formal dimension of the game—is what gives pleasure. In calling the strategic relations of power within S/M a convention of pleasure, Foucault appears to be suggesting that pleasure in S/M is the result of the insertion of master-slave relations into the framework of a game, that it is not inherent in those relations (and so could be absent from Nazism). Dominance and submission become sources of pleasure when they are aestheticized, chosen as the conventions needed by the game in order to make itself concrete. Indeed, the political rescue of S/M depends on this willed secondariness of the power structures it performs. If those structures were themselves seen as the principal source of pleasure, then the racial ideology motivating their adoption in Nazism would have to be recognized as irrelevant to their *erotic* appeal—just as their aestheticizing in S/M would be unable to account both for their position as the consistently privileged convention and for the excitement that convention generates.

Foucault's theoretical sleight-of-hand fails, in short, to explain why this particular convention serves the pursuit of pleasure so well; it is as if its choice in S/M were also an accident. S/M, far from dissociating itself from a fascistic master-slave relation, actually confirms an identity between that relation and its own practices. It removes masters and slaves from economic and racial superstructures, thus confirming the eroticism of the master-slave configuration. It is of course true that, outside such extreme situations as police- or terrorist-sponsored scenarios of torture, this configuration is, in the modern world, seldom visible in the archaic form of face-to-face relations of command and violation. Power in civilized societies has become systemic, mediated through economy, law, morality. But this hardly means that S/M is not a repetition of the power informing (giving form to) all such mediations. It is a kind of X-ray of power's body, a laboratory testing of the erotic potential in the most oppressive social structures. S/M fortifies those structures by suggesting that they have an appeal independent of the political ideologies that exploit the appeal, thus further suggesting the intractability of extreme forms of oppression, their probable resurgence even if the political conditions that nourish them were to be eliminated.

This could be the beginning of an important new political critique, one that would take intractability into account in its rethinking and remodeling of social institutions. But S/M's celebration of master and slave renders it (on the whole involuntarily) complicit with the perpetuation of regimes that promote the erotic opportunities of domination and enslavement even though, in a final twist, it should also be noted that S/M's perhaps useful demonstration of the need for such opportunities would be weakened were it to distance itself from the demonstration. By singing the praises of enslavement and torture, S/M self-sacrificially warns us of their profound appeal—self-sacrificially because S/M itself might not survive an antifascist rethinking of power structures. S/M, in a manner consistent with its most profound dynamic, couples its aggressive social posture with a hard logic aimed at its own immolation.

S/M profoundly—and in spite of itself—argues for the continuity between political structures of oppression and the body's erotic economy. Those practitioners and defenders of S/M who, like Foucault, would reject a politics grounded in brute force implicitly propose a kind of derealization of authoritarian structures. It is as if, recognizing the powerful appeal of those structures, their harmony with the body's most intense pleasures, they were suggesting that we substitute for history a theatricalized imitation of history. If, in one sense, this theater changes nothing and imagines nothing new, in another sense it changes everything: in S/M we can step out of the roles whenever we like. Since S/M shares the dominant culture's obsession with power, it simply asks that culture to consider exercising power in contexts where roles are not fixed and no one is really or permanently harmed. It proposes, that is, playing with power. The trouble with this is that if bondage, discipline, and pain are such extraordinary sources of pleasure, very few people will be willing to limit the enjoyment of that pleasure to weekend parties. Foucault curiously thought of S/M as an ally in the defantasizing of bodily pleasures, and therefore in contributing to that *art de vivre* he identified with killing off psychology. But sadomasochism is nothing but psychology. With its costumes, its roles, its rituals, its theatricalized dialogue, S/M is the extravagantly fantasmatic logos of the psyche. The somewhat poignant—and, it seems to me, wholly chimerical—proposal it makes is that we remove fantasy from history. It generously offers us its playrooms—in the charming illusion that, once having left the playroom, we will give up the pleasures that S/M has helped us to recognize as irresistible.

Perhaps S/M's most valuable lesson can best be approached through what most people undoubtedly consider its most repellent aspect: the inflicting of pain. Not too surprisingly, S/M texts are often evasive on the subject. Public relations probably lead the initiates to downplay the more shocking sides of their erotic fun. (The case for S/M would, ideally, be persuasive to those who limit their bedtime frolics to vanilla sex—hardly an easy task in a society where a limited sexual imagi-

nation can pass as a certificate of high morals.) Here is
Juicy Lucy's list of what S/M is and is not, in a volume
of essays from SAMOIS, a lesbian-feminist S/M group:

> S/M is not: abusive, rape, beatings, violence, cruelty,
> power-over, force, coercion, non-consensual, unimpor-
> tant, a choice made lightly, growth blocking, boring.
>
> Now a list of things S/M is: passionate, erotic,
> growthful, consensual, sometimes fearful, exorcism,
> reclamation, joyful, intense, boundary-breaking, trust-
> building, loving, unbelievably great sex, often hilari-
> ously funny, creative, spiritual, integrating, a develop-
> ment of inner power as strength.

If S/M has any specificity at all, it certainly includes,
however consensual all this may be, "beatings, violence, cruelty, power-over, force," whereas from Juicy
Lucy's happy list you'd never know that, as she writes
a few pages later, her toys include whips, leather wrist
and ankle restraints, handcuffs, and "some chain."[21] In
other texts, the emphasis on communal male jolliness
is such that you might think a Rotary Club promo-
tional piece had been mistakenly inserted in a volume
on leatherfolk. Little did I suspect, in making this comparison, that it had already been made, seriously, by a
dyed-in-the-wool S/M'er. Why, John Preston writes,

> should we be surprised by the emergence of gay leather
> clubs when for all practical purposes they're composed
> of the same men in racial, class, and economic terms as
> Rotary and Lions in the straight world? If you've ever
> been to a meeting of a leather organization and seen its
> nationalistic bent, patriotic fervor, and reliance on rit-

ual with the singing of common songs, and the pomp
and circumstance of its hierarchy, you can see that the
need being fulfilled is strikingly similar to what's going
on at any other men's civic benevolent society.[22]

When the subject of pain is directly addressed, it is
generally either in biochemical terms or through mys-
tical descriptions of the "cosmic ecstasy" induced by
torture. The biochemical discourse operates, interestingly,
as an indirect critique of the very categories of sadism
and masochism, categories that assume a transgression
of the pleasure-pain opposition they might seem to support. Mains writes about the metamorphosis of pain
into pleasure as a result of "the release of opioids in the
brain, the spinal chord, and possible into the blood-
stream," a process that seems to generate, "like a sud-
den fix of heroin . . . an ecstatic response and the abil-
ity to sustain, if not demand, increasingly larger volleys
of painful experience." From this perspective, the presumed identity of pleasure and pain in masochism, and
therefore perhaps masochism itself, become meaning-
less. The pain so-called masochists enjoy is actually
pleasure. They have simply found ways to transform
stimuli generally associated with the production of pain
into stimuli that set off intense processes identified as
pleasurable. Far from enjoying pain, masochists have
developed techniques to bypass pain; the chemicals released through S/M, Mains writes, "not only suppress
pain but also generate feelings of euphoria."[23] So the
psychological category of masochism is superfluous. The
masochist, like everyone else, pursues only pleasure.

If there is anything that needs to be accounted for in

masochism, it is not a supposed identity of pain and pleasure, but rather a passion for pleasure so intense that extreme pain is momentarily tolerated (rather than loved for its own sake) as necessary to bring the masochist to that biochemical threshold where painful stimuli begin to produce pleasurable internal substances. Masochism would, then, be an extreme hedonistic discipline. If masochists need to be accounted for psychologically, it would not be for their "unnatural" pursuit of pain, but rather for their potentially dysfunctional rejection of pain. For pain may be a signal that tells us to flee a stimulus threatening to the body's or the ego's integrity—to their coherence as securely delimited, individuating entities. Pain is the organism's protection against self-dissolution.

There is perhaps no way to give a satisfactory definition of pain independent of its protective function. The pleasure-pain dualism corresponds to a fundamental rhythm on the part of individual organisms toward and away from the world. A substantive (rather than functional) definition of pain always founders on the subjective variations in what is perceived and reported as painful or pleasurable. The subordination of pain to power in certain S/M discussions may correspond to an awareness of the futility, even the danger, of speaking of pain as an end in itself. Not only does that presumed end disappear both in its subjective variability and in the biochemical account of the blocking of pain; the exclusive focusing on pain can also obscure our understanding of the self-shattering which may be the secret reason for S/M's universalizing of pleasure.

In this self-shattering, the ego renounces its power

over the world. Thus, while images of Fakir Musafar hanging from the branches of a tree by hooks through his nipples (a photograph of this is reproduced in *Leatherfolk*) may encourage us to think of S/M as a kind of absolutizing of pain exactly identical to its suppression, it is perhaps not entirely disingenuous of Juicy Lucy, who describes her whip in some detail, to insist that "pain is simply the inevitable result of unacknowledged power roles."[24] Through pain, S/M dramatizes (melodramatizes) the potential ecstasy in both a hyperbolic sense of self and the self's renunciation of its claims on the world. The very aping in S/M of the dominant culture's reduction of power to polarized relations of dominance and submission can have the unexpected—and politically salutary—consequence of enacting the appeal of renunciation. The most radical function of S/M is not primarily in its exposing the hypocritically denied centrality of erotically stimulating power plays in "normal" society; it lies rather in the shocking revelation that, for the sake of that stimulation, human beings may be willing to give up control over their environment.

I am, of course, suggesting the primacy of masochism in sadomasochism. If there were such a thing as a sadism unaffected by masochistic impulses, it would reveal nothing more newsworthy than the pleasure of control and domination. The appeal of powerlessness would be entirely on the side of the masochist, for whom the sadist would be little more than an opportunity to surrender. Such surrenders obviously serve those who wield power in society: they certify the often voluntary nature of submission, the secret collaboration of the oppressed with the oppressors. But S/M also argues for the permeability of the boundaries separating the two. The reversibility of roles in S/M does more than disrupt the assignment of fixed positions of power and powerlessness (as well as the underlying assumptions about the natural link between dominance and particular racial or gendered identities). From that reversibility we may also conclude that perhaps inherent in the very exercise of power is the temptation of its renunciation—as if the excitement of a hyperbolic self-assertion, of an unthwarted mastery over the world and, more precisely, brutalization of the other, were inseparable from an impulse of self-dissolution.

It might be objected that there is very little evidence of any such surrender of power in the real world of dominance and submission whose structure S/M prides itself on exposing. The viability of that polarized structure depends on the successful resistance, on the part of the dominant, to the jouissance of self-loss, a resistance that in turn depends on a certain desexualizing of the sadistic position. This is not to propose, with Foucault, that Eros was absent from Nazism, although the efficiency of such social murder machines as Nazism may require a denial of Eros' presence. The complacency with which the powerful visibly enjoy their privileges suggests the relative success of that denial. And yet, given the apparent self-destructiveness of civilization, it could be argued—as Freud obliquely but powerfully does in *Civilization and Its Discontents*—that, on the scene of history, the promise of suicidal jouissance is what sustains the most aggressive self-affirmations and self-promotions. S/M strips away defenses against the joy of self-dissolution; in more general historical contexts, the countervailing instinct of self-preservation drives that joy underground, buries it, so to speak, in proud displays of mastery. But as we have seen over and over again, with dispiriting frequency, the oppressed, having freed themselves from their oppressors, hasten to imitate their oppressors, as if it were in the position of dominance that the drive toward destruction—and, ultimately, toward self-destruction—could be most effectively pursued.[25] S/M makes explicit the erotic satisfactions sustaining social structures of dominance and submission. Societies defined by those structures both disguise and reroute the satisfactions, but their superficially self-preservative subterfuges can hardly liberate them from the aegis of the death drive. S/M lifts a social repression in laying bare the reality behind the subterfuges, but in its open embrace of the structures themselves and its undisguised appetite for the ecstasy they promise, it is fully complicit with a culture of death.

If, as many readers undoubtedly feel, Freud has been waiting in the wings since the beginning of this discussion, it is now time to bring him to center stage. This move may be predictable enough on my part, considering my critical bent. But is it really possible for anyone seriously interested in Foucault on fantasy, sexuality, and power not to engage him in a confrontation with psychoanalysis? Can anyone believe that such peremptory formulas as *l'Art de vivre c'est de tuer la psychologie* make any sense except as an aggressive riposte to an interlocutor Foucault seldom acknowledges or addresses directly? He was so acutely aware of psycho-analysis as yet another episode in a history of discipli-nary networks that he never considered that psycho-analysis might provide some answers to questions he himself found urgent.

The first major theoretical attempt to desexualize pleasure was not Foucault's *History of Sexuality* but, about seventy years earlier, Freud's *Three Essays on the Theory of Sexuality*. It is that work which—forcefully, if evasively—first raised the possibility of dissolving the whole notion of sex in a reorganization of bodily pleas-ures. The *Three Essays*—to use verbs Foucault associates with S/M—already denaturalizes, falsifies, even deviril-izes the sexual. The passages in Freud's work that lead to his conclusion that "the quality of erotogenicity" should be ascribed "to all parts of the body and to all the internal organs"[26] could be taken as a gloss of Fou-cault's description of S/M practitioners as "inventing new possibilities of pleasure with strange parts of their body," and, more generally, of the call for a different economy of pleasures. The difference, of course, is that Freud continues to use the word "sexual" for a degeni-talizing of erotic intensities. Indeed, the originality of his thought has less to do with the pansexualism for which his contemporaries reproached him than with his appropriation of the notion of sexuality for certain phenomena that he was the first to describe and that have little to do with what had been understood until Freud as specifically sexual.

Freud coerced, as it were, the sexual into describing what I would call a certain rhythm of mastery and surrender in the human psyche. I think he was profoundly interested in studying how human beings both move to master the spaces in which they live (to take account of and to appropriate objects and other human subjects) and to renounce the project of mastery for the sake of pleasure. To survive in any environment requires a degree of invasive intent with respect to that environment; the exercise of power is a prerequisite for life itself. To note this was not original to Freud; the particular psychoanalytic inflection in a philosophy of power was the claim that the project of mastery might generate a pleasure—a thrill—incompatible with invasive appropriations. As I wanted to suggest in my remarks on S/M, political philosophies of power must especially take this rhythm into account. The psychoanalytic thematizing of the pursuit and renunciation of mastery as sadism and masochism gives a kind of ideal visibility to this double movement, which, however, sadomasochism performs reductively and melodramatically. Masochistic jouissance is hardly a political corrective to the sadistic use of power, although the self-shattering I believe to be inherent in that jouissance, although it is the result of surrender to the master, also makes the subject unfindable as an object of discipline. Psychoanalysis challenges us to imagine *a nonsuicidal disappearance of the subject*—or, in other terms, to dissociate masochism from the death drive. (My discussions of Gide and Proust in Chapter 4 should be seen as initial responses to that challenge.) In still other terms, can a masochistic surrender operate as effective (even powerful) resistance to coercive designs?

Interestingly enough, Foucault has a version of this double rhythm. It is decidedly nonpsychoanalytic: as power moves toward and against its objects, it inevitably produces frictions that thwart its movements. For both Freud and Foucault, although in very different ways of course, the exercise of power produces a resistance to power from within the exercise itself. Freud's version, it seems to me, gives the better account of the subjectivities that enact both the exercise and the resistance. The aggressive aim engenders a self-reflexive aggressiveness (masochism would be the *effect* of sadism). The subject seeks to repeat an excitement to which the object to be appropriated has become irrelevant and which may consist, most consequentially, in the dissolution of the appropriating ego. Appropriation has been transformed into communication, a nondialogic communication in which the subject is so obscenely "rubbed" by the object it anticipates mastering that the very boundaries separating subject from object, boundaries necessary for possession, have been erased.

The origin of the excitement inherent in this erasure may, as I speculated in *The Freudian Body,* be in the biologically dysfunctional process of maturation in human beings. Overwhelmed by stimuli in excess of the ego structures capable of resisting or binding them, the infant may survive that imbalance only by finding it exciting. So the masochistic thrill of being invaded by a world we have not yet learned to master might be an inherited disposition, the result of an evolutionary conquest. This, in any case, is what Freud appears to be moving toward as a definition of the sexual: an aptitude for the defeat of power by pleasure, the human subject's potential for a jouissance in which the subject is momentarily undone.

As I have been using the term, *jouissance* refers to an "erotogenicity" that, in the *Three Essays,* Freud ascribes not only to the body's entire surface and all the internal organs, but also to any activities and mental states or affective processes (he mentions intellectual strain, wrestling, railway travel) that produce a certain degree of intensity in the organism and in so doing momentarily disturb psychic organization. Following Jean Laplanche, who speaks of the sexual as an effect of *ébranlement*, I call jouissance "self-shattering" in that it disrupts the ego's coherence and dissolves its boundaries. (The jouissance that transforms sadism into masochism would also be an effect of such sublimated appropriations of the real as art and philosophy.) Psychoanalysis has justifiably been considered an enemy of anti-identitarian politics, but it also proposes a concept of the sexual that might be a powerful weapon in the struggle against the disciplinarian constraints of identity. Furthermore, as the writers discussed in the next chapter will help us to see, self-shattering is intrinsic to the homo-ness in homosexuality. Homo-ness is an anti-identitarian identity.

We might, then, think of sexuality not only as the strategic production described by Foucault but also as a good term to describe the nonstrategic effects of the body's exercises in power. Why should we do this? Remember that much of the appeal of sadomasochism for Foucault is that, as he says in the *Mec* interview, "with the help of a certain number of instruments, of signs and symbols or of drugs," it eroticizes the whole body, thereby desexualizing pleasure. This sounds very much like the nonsexual sadism evoked by Freud in

"Instincts and Their Vicissitudes," a sadism unencumbered by sexual excitement in its projects of mastery. It's true that Foucault speaks of these projects as erotic, and the distinction between the erotic and the sexual seems to be that the former is devirilized pleasure or polymorphous pleasure finally detached from the "virile form of compulsory pleasure which is jouissance . . . understood in the ejaculatory sense, in the masculine meaning of the word."[27] But in rescuing us from penile tyranny, from sexual machismo, these practices also bracket what may be—and here I can speak only of male sexuality—a man's most intense experience of his body's vulnerability. Foucault wrote so brilliantly of the body as an object of the exercise of power that we may fail to note how little he spoke of the body as an agent of power. What is to control or modulate nonsexual sadism, which in a sense would be the realization of the quite natural and quite terrifying human dream of an *undisturbed mastery* of the space in which our bodies move? The body liberated from what Foucault scornfully called the machismo of proud male ejaculation is also the male body liberated from what may be its first experience, at once sobering and thrilling, of the limits of power.

I refer to the experience of masturbation, a practice that Foucault saw at the very origin of the science of sexuality. What he called the war against onanism during the past two centuries was crucial in constituting the human being as a subject of sexual desire, a constitution that would be gloriously, or ingloriously, crowned by psychoanalysis. Freud is also interested in masturbation, but in a significantly different way. As part of

his demonstration of how each of the principal erogenous zones of childhood "leans on" a nonsexual function, Freud notes that the agent of masturbation is the
subject's principal tool for manipulating the environment: the hand. And implicit in this connection is the
suggestion that, to use another, coarser sense of the
word, the tool the little boy plays with gives him an experience of seriously qualified mastery: in masturbation
the hand produces an excitement indissociable from a
certain form of surrender, from, ultimately, a loss of
control. In masturbation the boy's body, more specifically the penis, disciplines the hand that would rule it.
If it is time to sing the praise of the penis once again,
it is not only because a fundamental reason for a gay
man's willingness to identify his desires as homosexual
is love of the cock (an acknowledgment profoundly
incorrect and especially unpopular with many of our
feminist allies), but also because it was perhaps in early
play with that much-shamed organ that we learned
about the *rhythms* of power, and we were or should
have been initiated into the biological connection between male sexuality and surrender or passivity—a connection that men have been remarkably successful in
persuading women to consider nonexistent.

Who are you when you masturbate? It is conceivable
that the body of another person would be able to excite
mine without hooking up to my fantasy network (and
that would indeed exemplify the irrelevance of predetermined positionings of desire to the production of
pleasure), but I find unimaginable a successful session
of what the disciplinarians know as self-abuse without
fantasy. We have, though, become extremely sensitive

to the danger of looking too closely at our fantasies. What positions, what activities, what identifications excite us? What imagined object best helps the masturbatory process along? What do we prefer the other to be doing—to us, for us, alone, with someone else? Such questions would of course not only be congenial to the confessor's forays into the penitent's soul; in more sophisticated form, they nourish the psychoanalytic curiosity about the identificatory moves of desire. The danger is clear. It is but a step from identifications to identity, and the tracing of the former's mobility may conceal an urge to find the common denominator that would, for example, definitively distinguish homosexual from heterosexual desire. It is after all Freud—with his confusing picture of inversion's genealogy in the first few pages of the *Three Essays,* especially in footnotes added in 1910, 1915, and 1920—who can be considered the first pluralizer of homosexuality. This does not necessarily make Freud more palatable to queer thinkers suspicious of all psychoanalytic investigations; his dismissal of the reductive view of male homosexuality as a woman's soul imprisoned in a man's body could be seen less as a rejection of essentializing than as a recognition of that particular definition's inability to cover all the subessences. Multiple typologies do not adequately justify the typologizing enterprise itself.

But how free do we become by freeing ourselves from typologies, genealogies, and schemes of desire, and are such schemes necessarily essentializing? Historically, there is no reason to find the answers to these questions self-evident. If, for example, we follow Foucault's and David Halperin's studies of ancient Greece, we see that sexuality was for the Greeks just as expressive of "the agent's individual essence" as it may be for us. Ancient sexual typologies, Halperin writes, "generally derived their criteria for categorizing people not from sex but from gender: they tended to construe sexual desire as normative or deviant according to whether it impelled social actors to conform to or to violate their conventionally assigned gender roles." This meant, specifically, not only that phallic penetration of another person's body expressed sexual activity and virility, while being penetrated was a sign of passivity and femininity, but, even more, that "the relation between the 'active' and the 'passive' sexual partner is thought of as the same kind of relation as that obtaining between social superior and social inferior. 'Active' and 'passive' sexual roles are therefore necessarily isomorphic with superordinate and subordinate social status."[28]

The nature of the agent's desire was, according to this analysis, more significant than the object of that desire in determining his identity—but the link between sexuality and identity was just as firmly established as it is for us. Indeed, the emphasis on what a man did instead of whom he chose made for an extraordinarily brutal reduction of the person to his or her sexual behavior. The male citizen did the penetrating, which was the sexual manifestation of something I see no reason not to call the citizen-essence. There is no escape from this judgment—no appeal, say, to the ambivalences of desire in order to prove (since such proof was necessary) that you were more virile than your passive behavior suggested. The Greek model is not only, as Halperin acknowledges, puritanical about virility; it is a striking example of the misogyny inherent in homo-phobia, even though it was not opposed to homosexu-ality per se. In a sense, the Greeks were so open about their revulsion to what they understood as female sexu-ality, and so untroubled in their thinking about the relation between power and phallic penetration, that they didn't need to pretend, as nineteenth-century sexolo-gists did, that men who went to bed with other men were all secretly women. Only half of them were women, and that judgment had enormous social implications; the adult male citizen who allowed himself to be pene-trated, like inferior women and slaves, was politically disgraced. The persistence of this judgment throughout the centuries and in various cultures is well documented. Foucault notes its continuing force even in contempo-rary gay life when, in the remark I quoted earlier, he says that S/M could help to break down a view among gay men that passive sex is demeaning. In short, it is not at all certain that the essentializing of a homosex-ual identity puts into effect a more rigid identity system than the one already in place—a system that didn't even have to be curious about the most minute moves of a man's desires in order to classify him ethically and to position him politically.

Even the crudest identity mongering leaves us freer than that. To be a woman in a man's body is certainly an imprisoning definition, but at least it leaves open the possibility to wonder, as Freud did, about the vari-ous desiring positions a woman might take. She might awaken in the male body the wish to be phallically penetrated, but she might also lead him to love himself actively through a boy (as, according to Freud, Leonardo sought to relive his mother's love for him as a child by becoming attached to younger men); or she might awaken in him a complex scenario of orality in which his homosexuality would, strangely enough, be best satisfied with a lesbian. The mobility of desire defeats the project of fixing identity by way of a science of desires. The gender system itself, as I said in Chapter 2, provides a basis for moving beyond the constraints and divisions instituted by that system. Historically, the invention of the homosexual as a type may have helped to break down the sexism in the earlier classifications according to acts alone. The *attempt* to essentialize homosexuality initiated an inquiry into the nature of the desires that impel us, say, to seek to penetrate or be penetrated by another person, an inquiry that must ultimately destroy any unquestioned correlation between the acting out of those desires and attributions of moral and political superiority and inferiority.

I have always been fascinated—at times terrified—by the ruthlessly exclusionary nature of sexual desire. Much of the interest of Proust for me lies in the self-lacerating candor with which he never tires of exposing that same fascination and terror in himself. This exposure involves a double humiliation: it is at once a confession of rebuffed desire and a narrative of the impressively base ruses by which the rebuffed lover seeks to exercise power over those indifferent to his desires. In today's climate of moral self-congratulation, which pits our own caring and nurturing queer selves against a vicious heterosexist community, nothing could be more unwelcome than the Proustian suggestion that the struggle for power unleashed by sexual desire may not be entirely the consequence of inequitable social arrangements but is a rather nasty aspect of the inescapable resistance the world opposes to our equally inescapable invasive projects. Given that nastiness, and the terror on both sides, we might begin tracing a theory of love based not on our assertions of how different and how much better we are than those who would do away with us (because we are neither that different nor that much better), but one that would instead be grounded in the very contradictions, impossibilities, and antagonisms brought to light by any serious genealogy of desire.

I want to suggest one of the ways in which sentiments and conduct we might wish to associate with love can emerge as a resistance, in the Foucauldian sense, to the violence and avidity for power inherent in all intimate negotiations between human beings. I will do this by looking briefly at one of the most morbid genealogies of homosexual desire in psychoanalytic literature: Freud's account of the origin of castration anxiety in the case of the Wolf Man.

On the basis of a dream that Freud's adult patient recalls having had at the age of four, Freud reconstructs an actual scene (he will in fact spend much of the case history debating with himself over the real or imagined nature of this scene) that took place when the boy was only one and a half years old. He had awakened from an afternoon nap in his parents' bedroom to see them engaged in *coitus a tergo;* both his father's penis and his mother's genitals were clearly visible in this rear view. The reactivation of the scene by the four-year-old's dream leads to a repression of the boy's longing for sexual satisfaction from his father, for it shows or reminds him, Freud argues, that the necessary condition of any such satisfaction—so the child presumably concluded from his interpretation of his penis-less mother being penetrated by his father—was castration.

But the strangest part of this interpretation of an admittedly doubtful (unremembered and constructed) scene is how little it corresponds both to Freud's own construction and to his account of the version given by his patient. First of all, the Wolf Man tells his analyst that "the expression of enjoyment which he saw on his mother's face did not fit in with [the assumption that he was witnessing an act of violence]; he was delighted to recognize that the experience was one of gratification." More important, nothing in the evidence presented suggests that the four-year-old resurrects his relation to his father in the sex act as one of terror. In fact, both the four-year-old and the presumably traumatized tiny observer of parental coitus display remarkably tender paternal feelings toward Freud's dreaded castrating father. When, soon after the traumatic dream, the little Wolf Man develops a compulsive interest in religion, he resents the God who let his son die because it seems to threaten the relation between him and his own father: "the God whom religion forced upon him was not a true substitute for the father whom he had loved and whom he did not want to have stolen from him." This resistance to a cruel God is by no means only a self-protective effort to save himself from Jesus' fate. In seeking to distinguish his father from that cruel and punishing Father of Christianity, the boy was trying, Freud writes, "to defend his father against the God"— as if he generously wished to save his father from being contaminated by an evil character, from becoming someone who not only might punish him, but whom he could no longer love. The child's affection was strengthened when, during the period of his religious conflicts, he visited his sick father in a sanatorium and "felt very sorry for him." Freud notes not that this "attitude of compassion" diminished the original terror of castration, but that it "derived from a particular detail of the primal scene"—that is, compassion for the father was, from the very beginning, part of that scene as Freud and the Wolf Man remembered or constructed it together.[29]

What was that detail? The Wolf Man tells Freud that while watching his parents make love "he had observed [his father's] penis disappear, that he had felt compassion for his father on that account, and had rejoiced at the reappearance of what he thought had been lost." Then, in the midst of all this, the one-and-a-half-year-old suddenly passes a stool, which event Freud interprets as giving the child "an excuse for screaming" and drawing attention to himself. But, considering what Freud says here and elsewhere about feces as gifts, we might also think of this as the little boy's attempt to compensate his father for his loss. The primal scene originates not only the threat of power but also its transference, its reciprocity. The view of the father as the agent of castration seems all the more mysterious when we recall having already learned—and Freud explicitly reminds us of it—that "the threats or hints of castration which had come [the little Wolf Man's] way had emanated from women." But no amount of evidence will deter Freud from giving the father the dubious privilege of exercising his castrating prerogative. If the child failed to read his father in that way, then this case history must be simply erased and replaced by phylogenetic truth: "In spite of everything," Freud asserts in one of the most remarkable passages in his work, "it was his father from whom in the end he came to fear castration. In this respect heredity triumphed over accidental experience; in man's prehistory it was unquestionably the father who practiced castration as a punishment and who later softened it down into circumcision."[30] For Freud, that decidedly nongay daddy, nothing would block the theoretical confirmation of murderous relations among men—an imperative undoubtedly based on the still deeper need to keep the sexes distinct and, in the service of that need, to warn that castration is the precondition of femininity.

But Freud's insistence on castration as the (fantasized) consequence of sexual satisfaction from the father is, as we have seen, resisted by his own account of the fantasies connected with that satisfaction. The case of the Wolf Man is a fascinating model of frictional confrontations: the real or constructed primal scene explaining or correcting the terror generated by the dream; the presumed fear of castration leading to a repression of desire for the father; the father's vulnerability as the *child's* resistance to his fantasized violence (or, alternatively, the father's violence as the child's defense against what frightens him in the father's vulnerability); Freud's interpretive violence against the evidence he himself records of the secondary role of castration in the child's (remembered or constructed) reading of a (remembered or constructed) scene of parental sex. The study is also dominated by powerful thrusts: the repeated penetrations of the father's penis; the interpretive aggressions of Freud's insistent, curiously unsupported theory of castration. But just as those potentially damaging penile thrusts meet what might be called the resistance of the child's solicitude, so Freud's resolute presentation of the father as castrator is effectively turned back by all the "memories" of the child's concern for the father's loss of power. In the Wolf Man case, a terrifying scenario of the relation between father and son as one in which the two are permanently separated, polarized, by a threat of violence that forces the repression of love is then partially rewritten as an account of a gentler exchange between the two, one in which the son's power is improvised as a response to the vulnerability inherent in the very position and exercise of power.

For us, perhaps better readers of the Wolf Man's story than Freud himself (who does, however, mention in passing that this case is the "furthest and most intimate expression of homosexuality"[31]), that story unintentionally provides us with one genealogy of gay love. We might imagine that a man being fucked is generously offering the sight of his own penis as a gift or even a replacement for what is temporarily being "lost" inside him—an offering not made in order to calm his partner's fears of castration but rather as the gratuitous and therefore even lovelier protectiveness that all human beings need when they take the risk of merging with another, of risking their own boundaries for the sake of self-dissolving extensions. If there is no fantasy to read behind the happy faces of those two gays we began by observing, perhaps there were, supporting their lovemaking, the shadowy figures of the loving child and the daddy he coaxed out of his terrorizing and terrorized castrating identity, figures who may have helped *them,* Foucault's couple, to spend a night of penile oblation.

4

The Gay Outlaw

Should a homosexual be a good citizen? It would be difficult to imagine a less gay-affirmative question at a time when gay men and lesbians have been strenuously trying to persuade straight society that they can be good parents, good soldiers, good priests. Though I find none of these options particularly stimulating, we should certainly defend people's rights to serve whatever worthy or unworthy cause inspires them. And yet, given the rage for respectability so visible in gay life today, some useful friction—and as a result some useful thought—may be created by questioning the compatibility of homosexuality with civic service. So I will begin my discussion of Gide's *Immoralist* by asking that question, just as Gide himself asks it on the first page of his novel.

"How can a man like Michel serve the state?"[1] For the character who asks this—one of three friends to whom Michel tells his story—its terms may be more ambiguous than the reformulations I have just proposed. What is meant by "a man like Michel"? What kind of man, exactly, *is* Michel? Perhaps in order to answer that question himself, Michel has summoned his friends from Paris to Tunisia. His wife Marceline has just died from the tuberculosis from which she had helped him to recover earlier. To what extent is he responsible for her death? They did return to the climate that had helped Michel regain his health, but their precipitous journey south—from Paris to Biskra, where Michel had discovered during his own illness how much he wanted to live—certainly hastened her death. Did they return to Africa for Marceline's sake? What has Michel himself been pursuing? For the reader of *The Immoralist,* the answers to these questions may be so obvious as to make the questions unnecessary. Michel, for that matter, is fairly lucid about his reason for coming back to Biskra. It was there that he met the Arab boys whose health and beauty awakened his desire to make his own body healthy and beautiful, and from his "unbearable sadness" in discovering that in just over two years those "lovely bodies" had been "warped" by "servile labors," he realizes that "*these* were the real reason I had returned to Biskra" (160–161).

The Immoralist, it would not be entirely unfair to say, is the story of a man whose discovery that he is a pederast transforms him from a prematurely dried-up bookworm into a passionate lover of life. One of the peculiarities of Gide's work is that this discovery is also presented as a secret. Critics, following Gide's cue, have frequently seized upon all the hints of Michel's pederasty, even though his taste for boys is crystal-clear from the moment, very early in the novel, when he notices the Arab boy Bachir's naked body "under his skimpy white *gandoura* and patched *burnous*" and leans down to touch the boy's "delicate shoulder" (22–23). Can this taste be a secret from Michel himself? However implausible that may sound, he realizes that he has returned to Biskra for the boys only after he is unbearably saddened by their changed appearances. Even more strangely, when little Ali's sister teases Michel about his preferring the boy to her, claiming "he's what keeps [Michel] here more than anything else," Michel, in the novel's final line, delivers what, for the reader, can only be an astonishingly belated, understated, and wholly superfluous confession: "There may be some truth in what she says" (171).

The fact is, he knows and doesn't know. While there are some things he knows (such as why he dragged Marceline back to Biskra), there seems to be something more fundamental about himself he still can't get to. If, he tells his friends, he has summoned them to this out-of-the-way place, it was simply to see and talk to them: "I need to speak," he says, "for I am at a moment in my life past which I can no longer see my way" (7). And, at the end of his story, he begs them to take him away from Biskra: "I can't leave of my own accord," but "I want to make a fresh start" (170). The temptation is to think of Michel's confusion as having to do with something more "interesting," more "profound," than his attraction to boys. And since most of Gide's

critics have been uneasy about his homosexuality, have
even felt that it obscures what is most interesting and
profound in his work, it has rarely seemed worthwhile
to resist that temptation.[2] I will, however, be proposing
that the profound interest of *The Immoralist* is Michel's
homosexuality, and that if the transparent secret of his
love for boys creates so much troubled confusion, it is
not because his guilt-ridden consciousness won't allow
him to accept his pederasty, but because he doesn't know
what he is in being a pederast.

In contrast to this unmistakable yet indefinable pederasty, Gide proposes—or may be allowing us to think
of him as proposing—a more conventional image of
homosexuality. With characteristic slipperiness, he invites us to think of Michel's male French friends as gay
men, even as he says nothing explicit to authorize that
assumption. The three friends have come to North Africa because of a pact made years before: "whenever
one of us called for help, the other three would answer." We know nothing about them except that they
may travel a lot (during Michel's last stay in Paris,
"Denis was in Greece, Daniel in Russia"), that in the
old days they often stopped their "loose talk" *(libres
propos)* when Michel, "the learned Puritan," entered
the room, and that they appear conspicuously free of
any spousal reference. In fact, they hardly appear at
all—except as a somewhat suggestive and slightly comi-
cal accumulation of men's first names at a couple of
points in the story. There is the narrator of the first few
pages speaking not only of Denis and Daniel but also
of Silas and Will (who "amazed" the other three with
their account of how much Michel had changed since

last seen in Paris), and, at the reception in Michel and Marceline's Paris apartment, there is this curious evocation of apparently unattached and casually insolent male guests:

> Antoine, Étienne and Godefroy, sprawled in my wife's delicate armchairs, were discussing the latest vote in the Chambre des Députés. Hubert and Louis were carelessly handling and creasing some fine engravings from my father's collection. In the den, Mathias, in order to pay closer attention to Léonard [are we expected to wonder what kind of attention this is?] had set down his still-smoldering cigar on a rosewood tabletop. A glass of curaçao had spilled on the rug. Albert's muddy shoes, shamelessly resting on a couch, were staining the upholstery. (101–102)

There is no way of knowing if these men constitute a gay coterie, and sensible literary criticism would in any case discourage speculation since, as textual creatures, they are of course nothing more than the passing mention of their first names. Structurally, however, they have much more weight, and their potential as symmetrical counterparts of Michel encourages us to speculate about them beyond what the text seems to authorize. If Michel's homosexuality is unmistakable but indefinable, theirs would be doubtful (*are* these gay men?) but perfectly recognizable. Here are gay men fully socialized, who can easily be called on to "serve the state." In society, they can be superficially irreverent (muddy shoes staining expensive upholstery, a cigar burning a rosewood table), but their naughtiness hardly makes them less assimilable or politically dangerous. Even Ménalque, the Wildean figure through whom we get a more articulate version of Michel's "immoralism" than Michel himself is able to provide, lives very comfortably within the society whose values he rejects. Having, as he puts it, no "sense of property," his Parisian house is a hotel where nothing belongs to him, but he has personal servants to wait on him and several rooms furnished as an apartment. Having been involved in "an absurd, a shameful, lawsuit with scandalous repercussions," he is shunned by Parisian society, but he also goes abroad on an assignment for the colonial ministry. On the occasion of that assignment, the newspapers that had recently vilified him can't find words enough to praise him for "services rendered to the nation, to all humanity" (103). The phrasing is significant: Ménalque, for all his isolation, serves the state. His "immoralism"— at least what we see or hear of it—is a philosophical and probably sexual idiosyncrasy quite compatible with a luxurious life in a nation he honorably serves. The only *denuded* figure in the novel is Michel, and if homosexuality is in some way linked to that denudation, to his longing for the "delectable company" of "the dregs of society" and his anxious need to get rid of his fortune (155), then we must look more closely at this curious sexual preference, which seems to require the repudiation of property and a renunciation of citizenship.

One thing is certain: this is a sexual preference without sex. Long before Foucault's unmasking of the classificatory processes that reified bodily behavior as psychic essences, Gide took one of those essences and rendered it, as a category, incoherent. It could be argued that the "authentic being" Michel searches for, "the man whom everything around us—books, teachers, family and I myself—had tried from the first to suppress" (51), is a pederast, but this has no sexual consequences in *The Immoralist*. All of Michel's behavior that can unproblematically be characterized as sexual (there isn't much of it, true) is heterosexual: once he sleeps with his wife, once with Moktir's mistress, and, apparently for a few weeks after Marceline's death, with Ali's prostitute sister. Michel's pederastic interests begin when he is ill, and what draws him to Backir (the first of the many Arab boys he seeks out) is his health: "The health of that little body was beautiful" (24). These modest beginnings in pederasty, far from bringing Michel into any relation with the boys, actually bring him to an unprecedented concentration on himself. He reaches for their bodies—in *his* body; they become a kind of sensualized ideal ego that beguiles him back to health.

The high point in this process of recovery is Michel's discovery, in Ravello, of the pleasures of nude sunbathing and swimming, pleasures that teach him what it means to be a *desiring skin*: "I felt the hard soil beneath me; the stirring grass brushed by body. Though sheltered from the wind, I trembled at each breath of air. Soon a delicious radiance enveloped me; my whole being brimmed to the surface of my skin" (56). *The Immoralist* is ambiguous about the authentic being Michel claims to discover through his recovery. The conventional way of thinking about this would be to associate that authenticity with a hidden profundity, and this is in part what Michel does. All the layers of "acquired knowledge" are stripped away, and there, buried deep within a consciousness invaded and falsified by culture, is the true self. But it is significant that when Michel speaks of this peeling away of the inauthentic, what is revealed is "the naked flesh beneath, the authentic being hidden there" (51). It is the surface that is hidden; the authentic is the superficial. It is as if the body had been buried from within: between Michel and his body are all the layers of acquired knowledge that have rendered the visible invisible. Now his body, uncovered, can *touch* everywhere. His authentic being—his naked flesh—extends itself into the world, abolishing the space between it and the soil, the grass, and the air. He *is*, briefly, the contact between himself and the world, and he has simultaneously become nothing but a bodily ego *and* has broken down the boundaries of that ego. Outside himself, he has lost himself. The narcissistic expansion of a desiring skin is also the renunciation of narcissistic self-containment.

John Berger has spoken of Renoir's landscapes with nude women as "an Eden of the sense of touch." Within the dappled skins "there is nobody"; the trees, rocks, hills, and sea beyond the bodies "prolong and extend the same paradise." All conflicts and differences have been eliminated; "everything—from the silicate rocks to the hair falling on a woman's shoulders—is homogeneous, and as a consequence, there is no identity, because there are no dualities."[3] Each woman is everywhere, and it is this very omnipresence that qualifies her massive corporeality. A potentially universal visibility reduces the visibility of an individual, bounded body. These correspondences of form, texture, color, and volume trace designs of sameness in our relations with the universe; our bodily being "touches" multiple other surfaces to which it is drawn, not necessarily by desire but perhaps primordially by formal affinities that diagram our extensions, the particular families of forms to which we belong and without which we would be merely the stranded consciousness hauntingly evoked by Pascal in the *Pensées*. Pascalian alienation is the separation of consciousness from the positioning of its own body within a universe of familiar forms. Michel's pederasty is the intersubjective figuration of these extensions. It is, so to speak, homosexuality without sexuality, desire that is satisfied just by the proximity of the other, at the most by the other's touch (analogous to the touch of the soil and the grass on Michel's body).

Gidean homosexuality is strangely undemanding, almost to the point of being indistinguishable from a homophobic rejection of gay sex. Gide thought of "inverts"—grown men who like to be anally penetrated— as morally or intellectually deformed, and it is one of the least attractive aspects of Gide's presumed defense of homosexuality in *Corydon* that the argument excludes what most of us would identify as homosexual desire. Gide's homophobia is regrettable, but the politically correct response to it—as well as to the offensive misogyny in *Corydon*—is probably the least interesting response. For his rejection, as a homosexual, of much of gay sex represents, in the form of a prejudice presumably motivated by moral principles, a view of intersubjectivity far more interesting and radical than those principles or even the sexual behavior that flouts them. A man being penetrated by a man is certainly not without its subversive potential: nothing is more threatening to the culturally enforced boundaries between men and women than a man participating in the jouissance of real or fantasmatic female sexuality. But I want to make the admittedly peculiar claim that Gide's fastidious sexuality is even more threatening to dominant cultural ideologies. Not only does it play dangerously with the terms of a sexual relation (active and passive, dominant and submissive)—it eliminates from "sex" *the necessity of any relation whatsoever.*

We may be inclined to read this as a failure to recognize the other as a person, to acknowledge his or her real otherness. Michel appropriates the Arab boys' presence for his own sensualist luxury. It is easy to see *The Immoralist* as yet another example of the sexual imperialism—both gay and straight—practiced by European travelers to colonized African countries. And I don't mean that there was anything radical in the failure of these travelers to think of the Africans from whom they bought cheap and, to their minds, exotic sex as people with whom they might establish a relation. On the contrary: the superficiality of their contacts reflected a more or less conscious conviction of the inherent inferiority of these sexual partners. The natives were insignificant, to be used for the travelers' momentary pleasures. French visitors to Tunisia complemented their country's economic colonization with a generally untroubled sexual colonization. Gide was certainly not immune to colonizing impulses (as he himself recognized), and yet those very impulses were perhaps the precondition for a potentially revolutionary eroticism. By abandoning himself to the appearances of sexual colonialism Gide was able to free himself from the European version of relationships that supported the colonialism. Michel's nonrelational pederasty, far from being a touristic diversion, takes over his entire existence—without, however, losing anything of its uncompromising superficiality. Michel has no interest in the boys to whom he sacrifices his wife, and while this certainly indicates a profound indifference to their otherness, it also means that he demands nothing from them. His eroticism is uncontaminated by a psychology of desire, by which I mean that it is unaccompanied by an essentially doomed and generally anguished interrogation of the other's desires. That interrogation is at the heart of Proustian eroticism. For Proust, the sign of sexual love is the mentalizing of the sexual drive, a disastrous sublimation of the desire for the other's body to an always unanswered demand addressed to the other's consciousness. The Gidean homosexuality of *The Immoralist* knows no such demands, and its very emptiness constitutes a challenge to any sexual ideology of profundity.

If this challenge constitutes a political threat, it is because of the energies it releases, energies made available for unprecedented projects of human organization. There is, of course, no politically neutral psychology. Gide invites us to go one step further and to consider psychology itself as politically diversionary. Our complex views of intersubjectivity, nourished by an intricate consciousness of desire, have the effect of channeling our imagination of human relations into the narrow domain of the private. To give up that consciousness, which fascinates us, would be a great loss. Indeed, to renounce a habit so profoundly rewarding seems tantamount to renouncing consciousness itself. And yet implicit in Michel's "immoralism" is the suspicion that there can be no radical psychology of desire, that psychology itself—as an account of what happens between people—assumes the durability and the acceptability of the political spaces in which it plots our complex private stories. Intersubjectivity as we have come to prize it in western culture, with all its intensely satisfying drama of personal anguish and unfulfilled demands, is a reining in, a sequestering, of our energies. And if, as I have argued, psychoanalysis undermines its own claims to the control of personal identity, it also immobilizes the human subject in its persuasive demonstration of an irreducible, politically unfixable antagonism between external reality and the structures of desire. The limited efficacy of psychoanalysis when it is used as a tool of ideological criticism can be accounted for not only by the modest and politically insignificant audience it reaches (academic intellectuals), but also because of the inescapably conservative implications of any discipline that traces for us the intractability of human desire.

It would be immeasurably sad to lose the richness of our Proustian perceptions, to settle (if that is even possible) for an intersubjectivity cleansed of all fantasmatic curiosity. Michel asks nothing more of the objects of his desire than to share a certain space with them; his homosexuality is a matter of positioning rather than intimacy. Untroubled and unconcerned by difference, he seeks, in those beautifully healthy Arab boys, nothing more than to touch inaccurate replications of himself, extensions of himself. Pederasty in *The Immoralist,* like nude sunbathing, is the narcissistic expansion of a desiring skin, and it too works against the narcissism of a securely mapped ego. Potentially everywhere, attuned to the multiple correspondences between himself and the world, the Gidean homosexual is unidentifiable and even unlocatable. There is no "homosexual psychology" here, for Gide imagines homosexuality as a gliding into an impersonal sameness ontologically incompatible with analyzable egos. Such self-impoverishing self-expansions block the cultural discipline of identification. The possibility of Michel's being saved for the state depends on his friends' being able to identify him, and this is what his account of himself—designed, presumably, to do just that—makes impossible. His secret turns out to be that he has nearly disappeared into a "place" where there are no secrets. Michel's friends are psychological missionaries. They have come not to bring him back to France but to do exactly what we see them doing: to listen to Michel in the hope of bringing him back to himself, *to a self*—the precondition for registration and service as a citizen.

Michel's pederasty is, then, self-less. If his homosexuality strikes us as elusive, this is undoubtedly because it is a subtraction from his being. His sexual preference is without psychic content; there are no complexes, no repressed conflicts, no developmental explanations, only the chaste promiscuity of a body repeatedly reaching out to find itself beyond itself. Furthermore, with remarkable consistency, Michel realizes that his psychic denudation must also be a material denudation. His pederasty provides a sensual motive for an attack on all forms of property—on the self that belongs to him and also on all his possessions. In *The Immoralist,* this

self-divestiture is enacted as a willful pursuit of abjection, a casting away not only of possessions but also of
all the attributes that constitute the self as a valuable
property. "I had sought and found," Michel says of his
trip back to Africa, "what makes me what I am: a kind
of persistence in the worst" (162). "The dregs of society," he tells his friends, "were delectable company to
me" (155), and in Kairouan he sleeps amidst a group
of Arabs lying in the open air on mats and returns
"covered with vermin" to his hotel and the dying Marceline. That scene could be read—if, say, we adopt the
point of view of the friends listening to Michel—as an
ironic commentary on the earlier tableaux of the con-
valescent Michel sitting among the healthy Arab boys
in the public park and gardens of Biskra. The purity
has ended in filth; the sexuality, still not wholly acknowledged, at once expresses and exasperates itself in
a camaraderie with debauched and diseased bodies.
Not only that: nowhere is Michel's *difference* from the
colonized men whose lives he would share more evident than in his touristic identification with them. He
realizes this: "Here too [in Syracuse, where he sought
out the dregs of society] the brutality of passion assumed
in my eyes a hypocritical aspect of health, of vigor. It
was no use reminding myself that their wretched lives
could not have for them the savor they assumed for
me" (155). And yet "each man's worst instinct seemed
[to him] the most sincere," and he insists, as he tells of
his prowling in the slums of Italy and North Africa: "I
feel nothing in myself except nobility" (157–158).

There is no need to resolve these contradictory judgments; indeed, it is one of the strengths of *The Immor-*

alist (and one of Gide's strengths in all his work) that it asks more questions than it claims to answer. But we might in conclusion try out another view of Michel's radical slumming. In his psychically and materially stripped-down state, Michel could be seen as a threat to the state. His friends' mission is not merely psychological (to restore him to psychology); perhaps they not only have to save him for the state but also have to save the state from him. The mild sensuality of Michel's convalescence is politicized during his journey through Italy to Africa with the dying Marceline. His longing "to roll under the table" with tramps and drunken sailors aggravates his "growing horror of luxury, of comfort" (155–156). It not only makes him approach his luxurious hotel with an hallucinated sense of the words "No Poor Man Enters Here" written over its door (156; an echo of the warning Dante sees above hell's gate). Michel's puritanically prurient will to get to the most intimate details in lives of impoverishment and debauchery is accompanied by a kind of Christ-like or utopian militancy:

> Human poverty is an enslavement; to eat, a poor man consents to joyless labor, and all labor which is not joyous is mere drudgery, I thought. I would pay one man after another to rest, saying, "stop working—you hate what you're doing." For each man I desired that leisure without which nothing new can flower—neither vice nor art. (157)

That leisure prefigures a new society, one "liberated from works of art" (the Arabs "live their art . . . they don't embalm it in words"), a society in which vice might be reinvented *as* art. *The Immoralist,* it is true, has nothing specific to tell us about such a society. The renunciation of work from below would be nothing more than a disempowering of the worker if it were not accompanied by a reorganization of the conditions of work itself. Michel's itinerary does, however, suggest that if a community were ever to exist in which it would no longer seem natural to define all relations as property relations (not only my money or my land, but also my country, my wife, my lover), we would first have to imagine a new erotics. Without that, all revolutionary activity will return, as we have seen it return over and over again, to relations of ownership and dominance.

Michel's pederasty is the model for intimacies devoid of intimacy. It proposes that we move irresponsibly among other bodies, somewhat indifferent to them, demanding nothing more than that they be as available to contact as we are, and that, no longer owned by others, they also renounce self-ownership and agree to that loss of boundaries which will allow them to be, with us, shifting points of rest in a universal and mobile communication of being. If homosexuality in this form is difficult to know, this is because it no longer defines a self. At once much less and much more than a sexual preference, it may also, as Marceline perceptively remarks, "eliminate the weak" (150). But the way we live already eliminates the weak, and the familiar piety she expresses serves to perpetuate their oppression. Nothing could be more different from the strength of Michel's self-divestiture, from the risks he takes in loving the other as the same, in homo-ness. In that love (for want of a more precise word) he risks his own boundaries, risks knowing where he ends and the other begins. This is lawless pederasty—not because it violates statutes that legislate our sexual behavior, but because it rejects personhood, a status that the law needs in order to discipline us and, it must be added, to protect us. If Michel's immoralism defies disciplinary intentions, it also gives up the protection. And this should help us to see what is at stake in Michel's timid sexuality. He travels in order to spread his superficial view of human relations, preaching, by his anomalous presence among foreign bodies, a community in which the other, no longer respected or violated as a person, would merely be cruised as another opportunity, at once insignificant and precious, for narcissistic pleasures.

✦ ✦ ✦

Nothing, Proust suggests, is more unnatural than for sexual inverts to come together. I mean "unnatural" and "come" in all their semantic richness. Not only is forming groups not what inverts spontaneously do; not only do they feel revulsion in each other's company. More profoundly, a society of inverts is also contrary to the very nature of inversion, to what constitutes the invert's identity. Having come together, inverts are, according to Proust, compelled to see with disgust their unnatural selves reflected in the specular presence of their fellow inverts. And there is no escape from this in sexual pleasure: it is unnatural for an invert to desire another invert, and so coming together, having orgasms together, can only reinforce the disgust of their having come together socially. Indeed, if we see inverts together, we should always suspect that they have sought each other out in desperation. Like Jews, to whom Proust compares them several times at the beginning of *Sodome et Gomorrhe,* inverts, ostracized and oppressed by the society to which they desperately long to be assimilated, may at last find "a relief *(une détente)* in frequenting the society of their kind, and even some support in their existence." Or—once again, Proust reminds us, like the Jews rallying around Dreyfus—on "days of [great] misfortune," inverts will rally around one of their own, a victim who provides a rare opportunity for solidarity among those stricken with the "incurable disease" of sexual inversion.[4]

What could be more repugnant to our own pride in a caring and supportive queer community than this brutal negation of communal impulses? Proustian inverts constitute a "race," almost never a community. Still, while I will not be presenting *Sodome et Gormorrhe* as a model of gay cohesiveness, I will argue that Proust, for all his gloomy (and bitchy) assessment of gay groups, can initiate a skeptical reflection among gays today about the values we may be perpetuating in our hard-won community. Probably no one, to begin with, would dispute the role of "days of great misfortune" in the forging of that community. The consciousness born at Stonewall—which helped to move many of us from a community limited to hysterical campiness and furtive cruising to a less secretive and more politically aware version of gay grouping—was shocked into being by a spectacle that made, finally, the oppression that had long been the fate of gays inescapably and intolerably visible. More recently, the spectacle of AIDS has provided an unexpected rallying point—one at once wholly

unwelcome and communally fortifying. It is not the
easiest thing to admit, but Proust is probably right
about the role of great misfortune in coercing gays (like
Jews) into solidarity, in making it impossible, or at least
momentarily unacceptable, to go unnoticed as part of the
general (which of course means heterosexual) population. This is not a remarkable insight, however. Proust
deserves our attention for suggesting something far more
significant: the aversion of inverts to the society of inverts may be the necessary basis for a new community
of inversion. The self-loathing implicit in the invert's
reluctance to settle for the company of, and sex with,
his fellow inverts could lead to a redefinition of community itself, one that would be considerably less in-
debted than we now are to the communal virtues elaborated by those who want us to disappear.

But the disgust must first of all be worked through.
It is grounded in homosexual identity itself as Proust
conceives it. His conception leads him to reject the term
"homosexual," thus aligning him with today's most ar-
dent anti-essentialists. But the alignment can only be
temporary: if Proust's investigation into homosexuality
reveals that the word misnames the phenomenon it
purportedly describes, the Proustian correction itself
will be made under the aegis of the most rampant essentialism. It is not naming that is put into question,
but only the wrong name. "Homosexuality" can't describe the attraction of one male to another male if,
according to the popular notion that Proust appears to
accept, such men have a woman's soul. As others have
noted, this rules out the same-sex desire it claims to
account for. Homosexuality is merely an illusion; what

looks like a man desiring another man is actually a woman longing for sex with a man.

Having spied on the pickup scene between Charlus and Jupien, the narrator congratulates himself on his earlier impression of the usually hyper-virile baron's effeminacy. "I now understood . . . why . . . when I had seen him coming away from Mme de Villeparisis's, I had managed to arrive at the conclusion that M. de Charlus looked like a woman: he was one!" (637). This heterosexualizing of homosexuality is so powerful that it risks invalidating the very formula it illustrates: *anima muliebris in corpore virili inclusa*. The woman imprisoned within the male body—like a disembodied spirit seeking the incarnate form it has been unjustly denied—will at times become "hideously visible"—when, for example, young unguarded queens are "convulsed . . . by a hysterical spasm, by a shrill laugh which sets their knees and hands trembling" (643), or when, more poignantly if more improbably, the invert, spied in his bed in the morning, is betrayed by the very hair on his head:

> so feminine is its ripple; unbrushed, it falls so naturally in long curls over the cheek that one marvels how the young woman, the girl, the Galatea barely awakened to life in the unconscious mass of this male body in which she is imprisoned has contrived so ingeniously, by herself, without instruction from anyone else, to take advantage of the narrowest apertures in her prison wall to find what was necessary to her existence. (643–644)

To see that inscription is always, in Proust, an extraordinary revelation. The narrator's reaction to his discovery of Charlus's sexual tastes nicely confirms Foucault's argument about the fantastic promotion of sexuality, in the modern period, from a repertory of psychologically neutral acts to "the root of all [the subject's] actions . . . consubstantial with" his or her identity.[5] Charlus the Sodomite is the key that breaks the code to all of his behavior: "the transformation of M. de Charlus into a new person was so complete that not only the contrasts of his face and of his voice, but, in retrospect, the very ups and downs of his relations with myself, everything that hitherto had seemed to my mind incoherent, became intelligible, appeared self-evident" (637). But what is it that the narrator has learned about Charlus in discovering his sexual tastes, in discovering that he is really a woman? If "man" and "woman" are fixed categories in Proust, it is also true that they are nearly empty categories. More specifically, they are unburdened with an ideological psychology of gender. A male invert is a woman for only one reason: "there where each of us carries, inscribed in those eyes through which he beholds everything in the universe, a human form engraved on the surface of the pupil, for them it is not that of a nymph but that of an ephebe" (637). Everything the invert sees is stamped not with what the invert "is" but with what he lacks. Charlus "belonged to that race of beings . . . whose ideal is manly *(viril)* precisely because their temperament is feminine" (637).

A theory of homo-ness in desire, as I began to suggest in my discussion of Gide, will lead us to question the Proustian equation of desire with lack. But for the moment I want to emphasize what happens when vision is occupied by desire. There is no perspective on the real that goes untouched by desire; conversely, sex-

ual desire itself may be nothing more than the appeti-
tive form of the subject's painful consciousness of difference. It would be something like an appropriating
reflex, a gesture designed to bring into the self what the
self recognizes as alien. Sexual desire here is the *activity*
within an extraordinarily reductive economy of being.
The male figure desired by the invert spreads, like an
enormous, form-defining shadow, beyond the male body
until it contains the entire universe within its contours.
The invert is nothing but his identity as an invert, and
the world is nothing but a massive enlargement of the
image in the invert's eye.

The notion of gay identity can go no further: every
move the invert makes manifests that identity. The subject fails to find himself in the world (fails to find the
same) not because of an openness to difference, but
rather because it is only by eroticizing difference that
the subject can hope for, or fantasize, the "possession"
of difference, and the consequent transformation of
both the self and the world into exact replications of
one another. This is in Proust the heterosexual project
par excellence. It is obscured by the frequent performance of the project in a densely homosexual context,
but, as we have seen, homosexuality is nothing but
disguised or mistaken heterosexuality.

Homosexuality in Proust is thus at once essentialized
and heterosexualized, and nothing could be further from
the way we like to think of being gay or queer today. The
heterosexualizing of inversion condemns the Proustian
invert to a loveless life without even the consolation of
good sex. Inverts "are enamored of precisely the type
of man who has nothing feminine about him, who is

not an invert and who cannot love them in return." Thus, the narrator continues, the desire of inverts would be "forever unappeased" if they didn't buy "real men," and if their imagination didn't transform other inverts into real men (638). Or, as Proust puts it in a notebook from 1908, the invert changes an attractive queen into a half-queen, "vite croit demi-tante une tante qui lui plaît."[6] A "real man" would of course be one who has the form of a "nymph" engraved on the surface of his pupil. The invert's terrible misfortune is that he *is* a nymph, but she is invisible to the true heterosexual man, hidden within the invert's damnable male body. As for the pleasure inverts do after all take with each other, it depends on a useful misapprehension. The invert knows he is a woman, but the other inverts who pursue him, while secretly sharing this knowledge, respond to that which hides his identity, to his male body. Thus, the invert must say, 'I will never be loved by men who desire what I really am, and I will be desired only by those who share my desire, that is, those who want what I am not.' Happiness in this scenario is perhaps even more improbable with those who belong to the same "race" than with those on the other side of the great sexual divide: 'my fellow inverts, recognizing themselves in me, have to find my nymph-ness repellent, and yet there is always the delicious chance that the real man may pierce the deceptive and repugnant surface of my male body and discover the graceful nymph imprisoned within.'

Small wonder that the Proustian narrator describes the project of creating a movement to rebuild Sodom as a "lamentable error" (*erreur funeste*). At once dis-

gusted with his own female identity and enamored of
those who love him only because of that identity, the
Sodomite would do anything in order to appear not to
belong to Sodom, taking wives and mistresses in other
cities and repairing to Sodom "only on days of supreme
necessity, when their own town was empty, at those
seasons when hunger drives the wolf from the woods."
So much for a gay community, which would exclude
the very men desired by its citizens. Sisterly comfort,
and solidarity on days of great misfortune, can go just
so far. The imperious claims of desire for real men will
finally drive the invert from the society of his fellow
inverts, and, once established, Sodom would be immediately deserted, with the result, Proust concludes, that
"everything would go on very much as it does today in
London, Berlin, Rome, Petrograd or Paris" (655–656).

Once enacted, this extremely rigid scheme falls into
interesting trouble. First of all, we should remember
that the occasion of the narrator's discovery of Charlus
as a woman is a pickup scene in which the baron plays
the role of a man. It is Jupien who is identified as the
female, who had "thrown back his head, given a becoming tilt to his body, placed his hand with grotesque
effrontery on his hip, stuck out his behind, struck poses
with coquetry"; the narrator, worthy of Charlus in his
horror at all signs of effeminacy, finds all this "repellent" (626). From the perspective of the Proustian theory of inversion, it is not surprising that the encounter
is structured as a kind of mock heterosexual meeting
between a man and a woman, or that Jupien would focus
on the baron's male exterior, ignoring the woman and

transforming the *tante* into a *demi-tante*. But what is the baron responding to? Jupien is doing everything he can to bring the woman within him to the surface, but if Charlus is himself a woman he can't be desiring Jupien "la femelle" unless . . . Charlus is a lesbian. And then, given Proust's resolute heterosexualizing of homosexuality, we would have to say that Charlus the female invert is really a man desiring a woman, for it is only by becoming a lesbian that Charlus could become the man capable of desiring Jupien the woman.[7]

The very stringency of these sexual categories thus demands an incessant crossing over from one sex to the other, and it wreaks havoc with the boundaries that usually keep each category in place. For in Charlus there may be two quite different women: the one who has a "manly ideal" and desires the male figure he is not, and the other who, in responding to an effeminate male invert like Jupien, is revealing the man "she" really is by pursuing a woman. Or it may simply be that Charlus is not entirely a woman, and that the real man in him is responding to the feminized Jupien—as if it were only by taking the so-called virile role, by being a top with a submissive, coquettish male, that the baron can express his troubled or repressed heterosexuality. Finally, Jupien is responding as if Charlus were indeed a man. Is he, like most inverts according to Proust, tricking himself into believing that this *tante* is a *demi-tante*, or is he excited by the real (straight) man he divines in the baron, or is he simply responding to the male body in which, after all, male inverts present themselves to the world, and behind which the invisible real woman is hidden?

The Proustian dance of essences becomes even more
intricate when desire is complicated by jealousy. I have
been speaking of how the object of desire can initiate
a certain mobility of sexual identity in the desiring subject. This is of course only half the story: we not only
desire others, but we also desire their desires. By definition, the invert will not be desired by real men, who
are unlikely to recognize in him the nymph that filters
and eroticizes their perception of the real. This causes
the invert great and permanent unhappiness, but it does
not plunge him into the epistemological anxiety he feels
when he loves an invert who also pursues women—especially if those women love other women. Rather than
welcoming his lover's versatility (which I won't call
bisexuality, since physical desire is always heterosexual
in Proust) as a sign that he has found a real man, the
jealous invert is now locked out of his lover's desire. In
the relations they have with women, these special inverts "play, for the woman who loves [women], the
part of another woman, and she offers them at the same
time more or less what they find in other men." This
makes for a double misfortune. On the one hand, "the
jealous friend suffers from the feeling that the man he
loves is riveted to the woman who is to him almost a
man." This confirms the impossibility of happy love
between inverts: a lesbian is a more authentic man for
the loved one than his jealous lover, who he knows is
really a woman. On the other hand, he is also not a
woman, or at least he does not know, Proust suggests,
what a woman is, since he has never been loved *as* a
woman. Thus he "feels his beloved almost escape him
because, to these women, he is something which the

lover himself cannot conceive, a sort of woman" (645–
646). (This is the source of Charlus' terrible jealousy of
Morel—terrible because Charlus, unable to formulate
his anxiety, will find that his own jealousy "escapes"
him.) What could be worse? Here is a man who is
really a woman suffering from an incurable ignorance
of what a desirable woman is. The jealous invert's lover
escapes him both in what he desires and in how he is
desired.

The profoundly heterosexual bias in this Proustian
analysis of homosexuality is expressly thematized in the
heterosexual lover's jealousy of homosexuality *in the
other sex*. The anxiety about the other's desires is most
elaborately explored in Marcel's suspicions about Albertine's lesbianism. It used to be clever to read Marcel's troubled loves as thinly disguised homosexual pas-
sions: Gilberte is really Gilbert, Albertine is really Albert
(or Alfred Agostinelli, Proust's chauffeur). If what was
known about Proust's life appeared to justify these gender changes, they altogether missed the point of Proust's
experience of homosexuality, an experience that seems
to have required that he be reborn as a heterosexual for
his novel. When, in the remarkable final pages of *Sodome et Gomorrhe*, the narrator seeks to explain the
intolerable suffering caused by his discovery that Albertine knows Mlle. Vinteuil and her female lover, he
notes that he might be able to win her back from another man, whereas "here the rival was not of the same
kind as myself, had different weapons; I could not compete on the same ground, give Albertine the same pleasures, nor indeed conceive what these pleasures might
be" (1157–58). If Albertine does indeed desire women,

then in a sense she shares Marcel's desires—but what does a woman look like from within another woman's desire? And if the desired woman is also a Gomorrhean, the image on the surface of Albertine's pupil becomes even more difficult to conjure up. What relation can there be between the woman inscribed in straight Marcel's vision and the woman through whom a lesbian Albertine perceives the real? How to arrest an image of a source of pleasure in this hypothetically endless crisscrossing of sexual identities, rigidly defined and yet irreducible to recognizable persons?

Yet this mystery is really not "out there": the narrator locates the impenetrable otherness of Albertine within himself. Once he is convinced of Albertine's lesbianism, the only accurate way to portray her relation to him would be "to place Albertine, not at a certain distance from me, but inside me" (1154). So the desiring Albertine, the girl who could give Marcel the key to her very being if she were to let him hear "the strange sound of her pleasure *(le son inconnu de sa jouissance),*" may already be constitutive of Marcel's very being. In *La Prisonnière,* this assertion will be given the form of a general law: "As there is no knowledge, one might almost say that there is no jealousy, save of oneself" (3:392–393). So the internalized interiority of otherness may be, for Marcel, the experienced otherness of his own interiority.

Let's return, for the last time, to that figure traced on the surface of everyone's pupils. We should remind ourselves that, according to Proust, this figure does not appear only at moments of sexual arousal or amorous interest, but is permanently "inscribed in those eyes

through which he beholds everything in the universe."
In other words, a figure of desire energizes all our interest in the real. In *The Interpretation of Dreams* Freud
writes: "Thought is after all nothing but a substitute
for a hallucinatory wish . . . nothing but a wish can set
our mental apparatus at work."[8] From this Freudian
and Proustian perspective, desire could be thought of
as an evolutionary necessity—not only for the continuation of the species but for every individual life. By
eroticizing that which we are not, desire saves us from
the ecstasy of monadic self-containment. But it also
makes for permanent self-alienation. Narcissistic plenitude is incompatible with self-knowledge; we can know
ourselves (we can know anything) only differentially.
We infer who or what we are from what desire tells us
we lack. Indeed, identity is the erotic modality of a
lack. Since an ephebe is inscribed within Charlus' vision, he is really a woman. The identifications that
psychoanalysis has taught us to think of as forging the
subject's identity are manifested through the desires
"proper" to them. Identity is the negative of our desiring fantasies.

Albertine was always within Marcel; but he becomes
aware of her presence only when she disappears from his
field of vision as a desired object and a desiring subject.
How can he know who he is if he no longer knows
whom he desires? Her lesbianism complicates the symmetrical simplicity of heterosexual self-identification.
Were all to go well (which is of no interest to Proust),
the negatively self-identifying nymph within his vision
would be replicated in the flesh by an Albertine carry-
ing within *her* eroticized vision the desiring male in

whom Marcel could recognize and love himself. In this scheme, uncomplicated heterosexuality is narcissism at a distance. Between two inverts, as we have seen, things get messier: invert X may desire invert Y, but Y may recognize, with melancholy, the mistake within that desire: Y's male body rather than his woman's soul is being sent back to him, as his identity, from within X's desiring gaze. And for the straight man desiring a woman who desires and is desired by other women, the self-identifying process is wholly blocked. Even more anguishing than the puzzle of Albertine's identity is the unfathomable mystery of Marcel's identity; Albertine's lesbianism deprives him of what has become, at this moment in his life, his major source of self-reference.

Anecdotally, Proustian desire is frequently homosexual; ontologically, it is always heterosexual. The sexual dramas of *A la Recherche du temps perdu* metaphorize a fundamental relation between the I and the non-I, a relation in which the subject is condemned to sociality as the precondition for self-identification. The subject is *in* the other who remains irreducibly other even while s/he is the same, inaccessibly out there even as s/he inhabits the subject's innermost being. Through Albertine's suspected lesbianism, Proust represents this identity of sameness and otherness in Marcel's own desires; lesbianism is a relation of sameness that Marcel can only see as an unknowable otherness. If homosexuality is "necessary" in *La Recherche,* it is not because of its author's sexual orientation. Instead homosexuality, or more exactly an internal homo-ness, is little more than the ground of a universal heterosexual—or heteroized—relation of all human subjects to their own desires. Thus Marcel Proust the homosexual had to submit to the torture of being heterosexual for the sake of those "truths" that art enshrines. In Proust, the tragedies of love—and the biological sex of the actors is irrelevant—are heterosexual, that is, tragedies of *inconceivable* desire.

Still, these tragedies open us to the world. Furthermore, and by no means incidentally, desire is not merely a mechanism of self-retrieval; our appetite for self-possession would not be stimulated if the real were not erotically charged, if desire did not invest living in the world with endless promises of pleasure. The Proustian model also allows for a deeply humane and self-enriching (not merely self-confirming) curiosity about otherness. The compelling need to possess the other's desires initiates what Kaja Silverman, borrowing a term from Max Scheler, has analyzed as a heteropathic sympathy with the other.[9] Once Albertine has become a "creature of flight," the only way for Marcel to know her is to imitate the movements of her desire. Whereas an untroubled heterosexual relation allows the subject to ignore the other's otherness and simply to pick up a reflection of desired selfhood in the other's desiring gaze, the homosexualizing inflections of Proustian heterosexuality necessitate a leap into otherness, an ultimately defeated but nonetheless self-diversifying effort to perform the phenomenality of the other's desires. It is true, however, that this performance is not playfully conceived or executed; it is motivated by intentions to imprison, and Marcel's heteropathic forays into the desires of the women he loves are designed to reduce their hetero-ness to the reassuring image of himself that can be inferred from his desire for the other. Thus we might say that a certain homosexuality (more exactly, a homo-ness), far from being a given in *La Recherche,* is the secret teleology of its powerfully constructed and nearly invulnerable heterosexuality. The heteropathic *work* of the Proustian lovers is a project of erasure, one that aims to reduce the other to a repository of the subject's own representation.

Because of this, the Proustian dance of essences is only provisionally liberating. On the one hand, an essentializing division of the human into "real men" and, presumably, "real women" is installed at the heart of homosexuality itself. There is, on the basis of my analysis so far, no same-sex desire in *La Recherche;* the appearance of same-sex desire, Proust implies, should merely alert us to a biological mistake in sexual identity. On the other hand, the multiplication and crisscrossing of gender identifications inherent in this system defeats any cultural securities about what it might mean to be a man or a woman. The dizzying intersections of essences in Proust's work blur the boundaries that essences are designed to solidify, and the very positing of sexual essences is, as I suggested earlier, a requirement for a blurring of identities and a consequent unavailability to disciplinary judgments—an escape impossible under a regimen of sexuality that, for example, categorizes male subjects by what they do rather than by what they are. Proust's novel is probably the finest example in western literature of the potential *generosity* of the discipline of psychology. It shows us psychology nearly defeating itself as a regulator, pushing its investigations of the self to those limits at which interiority, hyperbolically affirmed, becomes unintelligible. In that unintelligibility, the person as an object of cultural surveillance almost disappears.

Almost: in spite of such inspiriting attempts, psychological analysis undoubtedly remains committed, in its discursive intentionality, to elucidating the structure of a person. Marcel's sequestering of Albertine in her family's Paris apartment is an attempt to imprison her within his consciousness as a readable reflection of himself. The fascination of psychology, and of psychoanalysis, is inseparable from the exhilarating and chimerical prospect of control. To a great extent, analysis creates the human it sets out to explore. Like all intellectual investigations, it is largely an imaginary enterprise, one that laboriously fashions within the object of study an image of the presuppositions and methods of the study itself. The miracle of Proust is that his essences dance at all; the purpose of Proust is nonetheless to arrange them in patterns that can be analytically circumscribed—in short, to prevent the objects of discipline from escaping the disciplinary design they were created to serve.

And yet, at the very moment Proust's narrator most insistently represents homosexuality as a distorted relation of difference, he also lays the groundwork for an authentic homo-ness. This operation will be suggestive about the possibility of a gay community, even though it begins by evoking a community of being to which sex is irrelevant. Charlus is not exactly Charlus for two reasons. First of all, he is "really" a woman, but, second, there are correspondences that extend him beyond his boundaries as a person. If the relaxed and affectionate expression on Charlus' face as he steps into the courtyard makes Marcel think of a woman, the baron's look also generalizes him, makes him almost disappear as an individual into a family identity: "no more now than a Guermantes, he seemed already carved in stone, he, Palamède XV, in the chapel at Combray" (625). Not only that: the passage is noted for its comparison of the meeting between Charlus and Jupien to the fertilizing by a bee of a rare orchid in the Guermantes' courtyard. The botanical analogy is, as Sedgwick has pointed out, strikingly inexact, opening "gaping conceptual abysses."[10] But it does contribute to an important contextual effect, that of depersonalizing, even dehumanizing, Charlus. Not only do he and Jupien remind the narrator of plants; he also sees in their cruising the prelude to the mating of two birds, all of which leads him to defend the analogies themselves as "natural," given the vast community in nature of which the human is only a part ("the same man, if we examine him for a few minutes, appears in turn a man, a man-bird, a man-fish, a man-insect"; 628). In nature, as in social history, identities spill over. We exist, in both time and space, in a vast network of *near-sameness,* a network characterized by relations of inaccurate replication. Accurate replication—the perfect identity of terms—is an attempted human correction of these correspondences, a fantasy of specularity in the place of correspondence. To recognize universal homo-ness can allay the terror of difference, which generally gives rise to a hopeless dream of eliminating difference entirely. A massively heteroized perception of the universal gives urgency to a narcissistic project that would reduce—radically, with no surplus whatsoever of alterity—the other to the same.

Might this be relevant to love between the sexes? For
one thing, a good degree of homo-ness in heterosexuality could go far to calm the fears that nourish misogyny. In the passage from Proust we have been looking
at, it is heterosexualized *homo*sexuality that is nearly
transfigured—saved, we might say, for a gay identity—
by extending the characters beyond a delimited individuality plagued with sexual misassignments, and into
other generations, other species, even into the inani-
mate. These extensions or correspondences invite us to
depersonalize the pickup scene between these two men-
women, to remove from that scene psychologically recognizable individuals and to replace them with members of the same "race." If we are right to find Proust's
references to inverts as a race redolent of sexual racism,
the term (which nothing obliges us to keep) could also
be thought of as referring us back to those correspondences just discussed. This has everything to do with
shared being and nothing at all to do with knowledge
of a person.

It is this common appurtenance that two men, or
two women, acknowledge in cruising. When a man and
a woman pick each other up, there is nothing they have
to recognize except the signs of a mutual desire; their
heterosexuality is, in a predominantly heterosexual society, assumed; it doesn't make them part of a particular community. When a man recognizes another man's
desire, he is also learning something about the other's
identity, not exactly what kind of person he is, but
what kind of group he belongs to. In short, he both
knows him and doesn't know him—which makes for
an ambiguous knowing that the Proustian narrator for-
mulates in negative terms when he writes that Charlus'

cruising glance, "accompanied by a word," was "infinitely unlike the glances we usually direct at a person
we . . . know or do not know" (627). They both know
and don't know each other: is it this spectacle of ambiguous knowing that leads the narrator, a few sen-
tences before the words just quoted, to qualify the scene
as "stamped with a strangeness, or if you like a naturalness, the beauty of which steadily increased"? In any
case, it is certainly this knowing and not knowing that
facilitates the extraordinary democratization of sex in
gay cruising, which the narrator celebrates, perhaps
unintentionally, in his moving if overwrought evocation of the universal freemasonry of inversion:

> a freemasonry far more extensive, more effective and
> less suspected than that of the Lodges, for it rests upon
> an identity of tastes, needs, habits, dangers, apprentice-
> ship, knowledge, traffic, vocabulary, and one in which
> even members who do not wish to know one another
> recognize one another immediately by natural or con-
> ventional, involuntary or deliberate signs which indi-
> cate one of his kind to the beggar in the person of the
> nobleman whose carriage door he is shutting, to the
> father in the person of his daughter's suitor, to the man
> who has sought healing, absolution or legal defence in
> the doctor, the priest or the barrister to whom he has
> had recourse; all of them obliged to protect their own
> secret but sharing with the others a secret which the rest
> of humanity does not suspect and which means that to
> them the most wildly improbable tales of adventure
> seem true, for in this life of anachronistic fiction the
> ambassador is a bosom friend of the felon, the prince,

with a certain insolent aplomb born of his aristocratic
breeding which the timorous bourgeois lacks, on leaving the duchess's party goes off to confer in private with
the ruffian; a reprobate section of the human collectiv-
ity, but an important one, suspected where it does not
exist, flaunting itself, insolent and immune, where its
existence is never guessed; numbering its adherents everywhere, among the people, in the army, in the church,
in prison, on the throne . . . (639–640)

We might almost see here a Queer Nation poised for
revolution—even though these improbable comrades
don't share a faith or an ideology, only a desire. But
this may mean, as Proust does suggest, that they have
had to devise new ways of coming together, ways that
may also explore the political possibilities in their particular mode of meeting for sex. What kind of social
cohesion and political expression might develop from
the knowing ignorance that brings two strangers' bodies together? The move from an invert's cruising to a
politically viable gay identity is one that Proust doesn't
make, although, in an unexpected echo of Gide, he does
sketch the outlines of a community grounded in a desire indifferent to the established sanctity of personhood. Indeed, the person disappears in his or her desire, a desire that seeks more of the same, partially
dissolving subjects by extending them into a communal
homo-ness.

Lack, then, may not be inherent in desire; desire in
homo-ness is desire to repeat, to expand, to intensify
the same, a desire that Freud, with a courageously con-
fessed perplexity, proposes as the distinctive charac-

teristic of the sexual in his *Three Essays on the Theory of Sexuality*.[11] The aim of desire grounded in lack is the filling of the lack through the incorporation of difference. The desire in others of what we already are is, on the contrary, a self-effacing narcissism, a narcissism constitutive of community in that it tolerates psychological difference because of its very indifference to psychological difference. *This* narcissistic subject seeks a self-replicating reflection in which s/he is neither known nor not known; here individual selves are points along a transversal network of being in which otherness is tolerated as the nonthreatening margin of, or supplement to, a seductive sameness.

Whatever value such speculations may have, it might be said that I am no longer reading Proust in making them. And yet the opening essay of *Sodome et Gomorrhe* is haunted by the idea of gay grouping. Having made Charlus and Jupien almost disappear, as they cruise each other, into their natural extensions (into genealogy, into the other sex, into other species), the Proustian narrator returns, in the subsequent general reflection on sexual inversion, to the reasons why even the most solitary inverts are eventually drawn into groups of inverts. To be sure, the narrator has little to say about such groups, and he is quite nasty to boot. In one sense such communities, based as they are on a kind of depsychologized knowing and not knowing, could hardly be of much interest to this builder of such a great monument to psychological, personal analysis. It is, then, all the more remarkable that in spite of the absence, in groups of inverts, of all that appears to define and give value to a cultural community, Proust also manages to point us in the direction of a community in which relations would no longer be held hostage to demands for intimate knowledge of the other.[12] In any case, if we are tempted to dismiss the Proustian reflection on inversion as regressively dependent on essentializing assumptions, it would be salutary to acknowledge that our own thinking about a radical queer community has not, so far, produced much more than demands to let us into the dominant community or, at the most, attempts to reconceptualize that community subversively. Proust—and Genet will make an immense leap in this direction—at least raises the possibility of breaking that tie, of repudiating the debt, and therefore of starting to think over what might be valuably human in the human community.

+ + +

Betrayal is an ethical necessity.

This difficult and repugnant truth is bound to be the major stumbling block for anyone interested in Jean Genet. Readers will sympathize with his biographer Edmund White, who confesses that he could never comprehend Genet's "purported admiration for *treachery* . . . I recognize that a prisoner might be *forced* to betray his friends, but how can one be *proud* of such a failing?"[13] Genet the thief, Genet the jailbird, Genet the flamboyantly horny homosexual: all this is acceptable, almost respectable, compared with Genet's dirty little confession that he handed over to the police his "most tormented *(martyrisé)* friend" and that, to make his act even more ignominious, to deprive it of any appearance of being gratuitous or disinterested, he demanded pay-

ment for his treachery.[14] There is no honor among thieves
here, none of that loyalty to one's brothers in crime
that gives to Balzac's Vautrin an irresistible moral appeal. (Vautrin could give respectable society a lesson in
the respectable virtue of loyalty.) Whether or not Genet
is telling the truth about his treachery is, for us, irrelevant; what matters is his rejection of any such appeal,
his refusal to argue that the criminal world adheres
more rigorously to ethical ideals than the "lawful" society in which those ideals originated.

This refusal only partially constitutes the much more
ambitious intention of imagining a form of revolt that
has no relation whatsoever to the laws, categories, and
values it would contest and, ideally, destroy. I referred
earlier to an important project in recent queer theory,
especially as formulated by Judith Butler: that of citing
heterosexual (and heterosexist) norms in ways that mark
their weakness in them—ways that will at once expose
all the discursive sites of homophobia and recast certain values and institutions like the family as, this time
around, authentically caring and enabling communities.[15] Genet can perhaps contribute to the critical rigor
of this project by providing a perversely alien perspective. He is basically uninterested in any redeployment
or resignification of dominant terms that would address the dominant culture. Not only does he fail to
engage in parodistically excessive miming of that culture's styles and values; it would also blunt the originality of his work to claim, as Sartre does, that his
embrace of criminality is designed to transform a stig-
matizing essence imposed on him by others into a freely
chosen destiny (as if he were stealing from the commu-

nity that has excluded him and saying, "Only I am responsible for the being in which others have sought to imprison me").[16] Let's test a more difficult position: Genet's use of his culture's dominant terms (especially its ethical and sexual categories) are designed not to rework or to subvert those terms, but to exploit their potential for erasing cultural relationality itself (that is, the very preconditions for subversive repositionings and defiant repetitions).

This erasure cannot, however, be immediately effected. The process does include certain reversals, or antithetical reformulations, of given categories. Betrayal, most notably, instead of producing guilt, is embraced as a moral achievement; it was, he writes in *Funeral Rites*, the most difficult step in the "particular ascesis" that led him to evil (80). But even here the reversal of value obscures the original term of the reversal, which is lost in what Genet insists, in *Prisoner of Love*, is the ecstasy generated by betrayal. Betrayal's place in an ethical reflection disappears in the immediacy of an "erotic exaltation," and this categoric displacement saves Genet's attraction to treachery from being merely a transgressive relation to loyalty.[17]

For Genet, homosexuality has to be implicated in betrayal once the latter is erotically charged. It would be convenient to separate the two (to take the homosexuality without the betrayal), but this reassuring move would miss Genet's original and disturbing notion that homosexuality is congenial to betrayal and, further, that betrayal gives homosexuality its moral value. In *Funeral Rites*, where these connections are most powerfully made, Genet writes that "love for a woman or girl is not to be compared to a man's love for an adolescent boy" (18). If betrayal is somehow crucial to the erotic specificity of homosexuality, and if "incomparable" homosexuality is defined not only as male homosexuality but also as, possibly, a certain relation of dominance and submission between a man and a boy, then the moral argument for betrayal risks being dismissed as a perverse sophistry. It is inferred, one might say, from a highly restrictive erotics, and the very possibility of making such an inference would be enough to discredit the sexuality in which it is grounded.

But the value of betrayal is a mythic configuration in *Funeral Rites,* and as such it has the universal particularity of all myths. It has been objected that the psychoanalytic Oedipus myth also describes a very limited situation: not only the fantasmatic anxieties of little boys (and not little girls) at a certain stage in their affective and sexual development, but also the fantasmatic field of the nuclear bourgeois family at a particular moment in European history, and perhaps also during a crisis in a patriarchal community structured according to an ancient Judaic veneration for and terror of the lawgiving Father. But these arguments don't invalidate the myth, and the truth of the Oedipus complex has nothing to do with its empirical correspondences, with the number of families that might recognize themselves in the oedipal triangle. This is a myth about triangularity itself, about the dependence of all sociality on the disruptive effect of a third agent on the intimately conjoined couple. The oedipal father is nothing more—and nothing less—than the voice that disturbs a copulative plenitude. It could of course be said that patriarchy has corrupted this necessary myth by asking us to believe that the voice delivers a terrorizing prohibition, whereas it *might* have been figured as a seductive invitation to substitute sociability for passion. This would be a superficial reading, however. If the myth's applicability is not restricted to families that faithfully reflect its patriarchal structure, that structure is nonetheless a privileged vehicle for the dramatic metaphorizing of the subject's *need* to be summoned out of intimacy and into the social, to be saved from ecstatic unions that threaten individuation. The prohibiting father is not, after all, external to the scenario of union with the mother. He does not invade, from the outside, an unambivalent attachment; he is a constitutive element of the attachment in that he saves the subject from the dangers of desire. He allows for the expression of desire by guaranteeing that it will not be satisfied. In somewhat similar fashion, pederastic male intimacies do not delimit the field of applicability for Genet's myth of homosexual betrayal, although perhaps only "the homosexual" can make the ethical necessity of betrayal intelligible.

Funeral Rites was inspired by the death of one of Genet's lovers, Jean Decarnin, a twenty-year-old communist resistance fighter shot down in 1944 on the barricades in Paris "by the bullet of a charming young collaborator" (17). The avowed aim of *Funeral Rites* is "to tell the glory of Jean Decarnin," but, as Genet confides at the beginning, the work may have some "unforeseeable secondary aims" (13). Indeed, a curious aim rapidly takes over: that of praising the murderous collaborator (Genet names him Riton) and, more generally, the Nazis who were Jean's (and France's) enemy. In other words, Genet mourns Jean through an act of treachery. "I have the soul of Riton. It is natural for the piracy, the ultra-mad banditry of Hitler's adventure, to arouse hatred in decent people but deep admiration and sympathy in me" (116).

We can deal quickly with the banal reasons for this betrayal, reasons that seek to justify it, thereby depriving it of much of its force. There is first of all the distance between the official language of elegy and the particular intensity of Genet's mourning for Jean. The farther Genet can get from the canonical solemnity dictated by death, the more convincingly personal and sincere his pain will appear—to him and to us. In the face of the clichéd piety of the notice pinned to a tree at the site of Jean's death ("A young patriot fell here. Noble Parisians, leave a flower and observe a moment of silence"), Genet's nutty fantasies of Jean's soul now inhabiting a matchbox in his pocket, or a garbage pail lovingly covered with flowers bespattered with filth when the pail explodes, testify to the originality of his grief, to that fierce refusal to let Jean go which inspires such cannibalistic fantasies as that of the hungry Genet, knife and fork in hand, greedily anticipating the taste of the skin and organs of the beloved corpse, salivating at the prospect of soaking the choicest pieces in their own fat. Treachery has a special function in this defiant rejection of the codes of mourning. Instead of allowing the code to stand in for him and be an impersonal witness to his grief, Genet will prove his grief to himself by the pain he feels at his betrayal of Jean. If, as he writes, it is only in losing Jean that he realizes how attached he was to him, then suffering should be cultivated as the most reliable proof of love. To treat the dead Jean treacherously is torture, so Genet must have loved Jean. The formula will serve self-knowledge in the future: "I would like to be an out-and-out bastard and kill those I love—handsome adolescents—so that I may know by my greatest pain my deepest love for them" (not in English; 68 in CI).

This logic, which is Genet showing off as a writer, is ethical kitsch. Betrayal as an original act of mourning is nothing more than a straining toward literary originality, and as such it is the least gripping idea in *Funeral Rites*. Much more interesting is how betrayal is inscribed within homosexual love itself. What appears to give Genet his best erotic high is the act of rimming. Here is a fantasy of Genet as Hitler with a young Frenchman (Jean's brother):

> Paulo's behind was just a bit hairy. The hairs were blond and curly. I stuck my tongue in and burrowed as far as I could. I was enraptured with the foul smell. My mustache brought back, to my tongue's delight, a little of the muck that sweat and shit formed among Paulo's blond curls. I poked about with my snout, I got stuck in the muck, I even bit—I wanted to tear the muscles of the orifice to shreds and get all the way in, like the rat in the famous torture, like the rats in the Paris sewers which devoured my finest soldiers. (139)

Genet's cannibalistic appropriation of Jean after his death turns out to be a continuation of their lovemaking. Genet was already "eating him up," and what he was eating was, so to speak, Jean already dead. It is as if, in his oral passion for his lover's anus, for the bits

of fecal matter clinging to the opening, Genet was ex-
pressing a preference for what his lover's body had
rejected, for what was no longer of any use to the living
Jean. In rimming, the other is momentarily reduced to
an opening for waste and to the traces of waste. Genet's
fantasy goes further: not content merely to eat what
Jean expels, he fantasizes transforming all of Jean into
his own waste. The foraging tongue inspires a dream
of total penetration, of entering the lover through the
anus and continuing to devour him at the very site of
his production of waste. Thus Genet eating Jean inside
Jean could himself become the expeller of Jean's waste
or, more accurately, the expeller of Jean *as* waste. (Or
perhaps Jean would expel *him* as waste . . .)

The violence of this fantasy is ambiguous: Genet's
excitement is murderous, but murder itself serves an ideal
of perfect identity between the lovers. Genet's attack is,
true enough, the treacherous transformation of a form
of sexual servicing into a serving up of the lover's entire
being. In psychoanalytic terms, the fury of anality (suggested by the image of the attacking rat) reinforces the
murderous impulses of orality. But Genet's amorous
attack also eliminates differences between him and Jean;
rimming is a symbiotic operation. He erases the difference between Jean and himself not only through his
fantasies of making a meal of his lover's corpse, but
also through his project of disappearing into Jean's body,
of being "digested" by Jean from below. Thus Jean
himself is fantasized as responding to Genet's oral cannibalism with a rectal cannibalism that devours Genet.
The two have become one, and the slight discursive
dizziness we experience in the constant references to
"Jean" and "Genet" as two is at least fantasmatically

cured when the specular relation of Jean to Jean is momentarily perfected as an identity between the two.

Sándor Ferenczi theorized that, in intercourse with a woman, a man seeks unconsciously to return to the security of existence within the womb.[18] Genet's fantasized ascent into Jean through his anus is a savage reversal of this coming back to a life-nourishing site in the mother's body. The "return" is now staged as reproductivity sterile; from another man's body, Genet can only emerge, or reemerge, as waste. Rimming thus replays the origins of life as an original death, both for Genet as subject and for the lover-mother. This death is relived both as fierce aggression and, in a parodistic reprise of the ecstatically sated infant slumbering at its mother's breast, as a lovely death within the "cool bower" of Jean's rectum, "which I crawled to and entered with my entire body, to sleep on the moss there, in the shade, to die there" (253).

So that "charming young collaborator" who killed Jean simply makes real the death at the heart of Genet's love for Jean. For Genet this dense network of betrayal and death—which includes ceremoniously embellished memories of rimming, a murderous ripping into the lover's entrails, Genet's discovery of his love for Jean only when Jean can be imagined as an edible corpse, a limitless tenderness for the traitor who in effect served Jean up to Genet as adorably and irresistibly lifeless— all of this documents, so to speak, the availability of homosexuality to Genet's ascetic pursuit of evil. Far from simply rejecting a homophobic emphasis on the sterility of gay love, Genet joyfully embraces what might be called the anatomical emblem of that sterility. Could it be this failure to produce life, the absence of a reproductive site in (and exit from) the male body, as well as the "wasting" of sperm in the partner's digestive tract or rectum, that makes Genet refer to the love between two males as incomparable?

These connections are overdetermined in *Funeral Rites* without ever being stated. The jouissance of rimming is escalated—one might also say sublimated—into a celebration of Jean's death and a passion for his murderer and his enemies. The pleasure of tasting Jean's waste is the pleasure of tasting Jean *as* waste, and this is to love Jean as dead, which is to will him dead and, finally, to make virtues of treachery and murder. These logically unjustifiable equivalences nonetheless have the "rightness" of an erotic crescendo, of an unreasoned yet irrefutable ratiocination of a very specific jouissance. The affective and ethical deduction to which this jouissance escalates—the amorous excitement in betraying Jean and handing him over, dead, to his murderer—maintains, as Genet says of betrayal in *Prisoner of Love,* the "erotic exaltation" in which it began. In Genet, murderous betrayal generalizes and socializes rimming without losing any of rimming's erotic energy. Genet's moral abstractions are not symptomatic substitutes for repressed sexuality. The sexuality in which those abstractions are grounded persists not under but alongside the ascetic pursuit of evil. Indeed, the practice of rimming could be thought of as periodically recharging Genet's ethic of evil.

This, I believe, is the intolerable moral logic of Genet's erotics. Nearly all his works relentlessly, floridly, celebrate homosexuality, and yet he is the least "gay-affirmative" gay writer I know. His demand that others find him hateful and unworthy of human society stands in sharp contrast to the tame demand for recognition on the part of our own gay community. This in itself, I hasten to say, would hardly justify the interest so many take in Genet—even though there is something salubriously perverse, especially today, in his refusal to argue for any moral value whatsoever in homosexuality. But so far I have been giving an insufficiently radical reading of his work. What we have seen him do is to renegotiate the values of given terms: he repeats society's accusation of him as a homosexual outlaw, meticulously seeking out every ramification, every implication of that accusation (much as his tongue industriously and lovingly sweeps up the waste around his lover's anus), making of a sterile, treacherous, even murderous relation to others the precondition of his sexual pleasure. But this still leaves Genet socially positioned. He is willfully offering transgressive spectacles to others, making himself into a gaudy performer of their most lurid views of him. This is the best-known Genet, frozen in fussily obscene, theatricalizing postures, Genet wondering as he writes if he has found the perfect gesture. Here the aesthetic frequently arrests the erotic by monumentalizing moments of fantasy, thus putting an end to the escalating movement just discussed. Genet's preparation of the gesture and the poses by which we can only assume he hopes to be remembered counters the mobility and destructiveness of his erotic energy. Through these tableaux he defiantly—and nondialogically—addresses society's interpellations of him.

More boldly than any other of Genet's works, *Fu-*

neral Rites raises the possibility of an escape from the
spectacular transgression itself, and in so doing it also
sketches an anti-monumental, anti-redemptive aesthetics at odds with his apparent pursuit of gestural beauty.
In his most original move, Genet imagines a kind of
nonrelational betrayal. This is all the more difficult to
perceive because it emerges from an old, familiar ethical discourse. The parameters of evil appear to be clearly
defined by the virtues that evil systematically flouts.
Genet's claim of having reached, through the ascesis of
his self-imposed training in evil, some sort of authentic
freedom is belied by the apparent dependence of evil
on social definitions of the good:

> Having chosen to remain outside a social and moral
> world whose code of honor seemed to me to require
> rectitude, politeness, in short the precepts taught in
> school, it was by raising to the level of virtue, for my
> own use, the opposite of the common virtues that I
> thought I could attain a moral solitude where I would
> never be joined. I chose to be a traitor, thief, looter,
> informer, hater, destroyer, despiser, coward. (170–171)

What kind of freedom is there in an evil that makes each
of its moves in response to an accepted virtue? The
threat of evil is considerably diminished when its entire
field is determined, and in some way controlled, by the
ethical arrangements it transgresses. Evil is already con-
tained within those arrangements; its destructiveness
could even be thought of as a necessity for the sake of the
good itself. The historical visibility of evil clarifies the
ethical foundation of the social; it imposes, at the very
least, a definitional reinforcement of those foundations.

But Genet is also aiming at something else, something pointed to by the deceptively banal notation that through evil one reaches solitude. I say "deceptively" because Genet doesn't mean that solitude is the consequence of evil; rather, he embraces crime *in order to* be alone. Indeed, to find company in evil, to be surrounded by people who "are as at home in infamy as a fish is in water" is enough to make him retreat into virtue (171). And of the traitor Riton, Genet writes:

> I am keen on his continuing until the last fraction of a second, by destruction, murder—in short, evil according to you—to exhaust, and for an ever greater exaltation—which means elevation—the social being or gangue from which the most glittering diamond will emerge; solitude, or saintliness, which is also to say the unverifiable, sparkling, unbearable play of his freedom. (160)

From these passages a new possibility emerges: evil (to continue using Genet's term) not as a crime against socially defined good, but as a turning away from the entire theater of the good, that is, a kind of meta-transgressive *dépassement* of the field of transgressive possibility itself.

It is here that homosexuality reveals to Genet its richest potential for evil. For him, this potential is always rooted, as we have seen with rimming, in a specific sexual practice. Once again, the anus will provide the privileged passage to Genet's highest sublimations. Anal intercourse, even more than rimming, is extravagantly developed for its most radical moral and political implications in *Funeral Rites*. It is of course true that neither of those practices is exclusive to gay men;

nor do they exhaust the possibilities of homosexual eroticism. But the frequency with which they are practiced is irrelevant; for Genet, they mythically emphasize the sterility of a relation from which the woman's body is excluded and—to anticipate my next point—the anti-relationality inherent in all homo-ness.

This discovery may be the result of a positional preference. *Coitus a tergo* is of course a heterosexual option; correlatively, two men or two women can make love facing each other. But Genet appears to prefer to approach from behind the sexual opportunity that *is* behind, as if the configuration of the front of one man's body against the back of the other most closely respects, so to speak, the way in which the anus (as distinct from the vagina) presents itself for penetration. It is in this position, as the following extraordinary passage suggests, that Genet discovers the inestimable value of sex without exchanges. The German soldier Erik fucks the young collaborator Riton on the rooftop of an abandoned apartment building where the two of them, along with some other German soldiers, have been hiding out during the liberation of Paris:

> Leaning back against the brick monument, facing a Paris that was watching and waiting, Erik buggered Riton. Their trousers were lowered over their heels where the belt buckles clinked at each movement. The group was strengthened by leaning against the wall, by being backed up, protected by it. If the two standing males had looked at each other, the quality of the pleasure would not have been the same. Mouth to mouth, chest to chest, with their knees tangled, they would have been

entwined in a rapture that would have confined them
(une ivresse qui ne sortait pas d'eux-mêmes) in a kind
of oval that excluded all light, but the bodies in the
figurehead which they formed looked into the darkness,
as one looks into the future, the weak sheltered by the
stronger, the four eyes staring in front of them. They
were projecting the frightful ray of their love to infinity
. . . Erik and Riton were not loving one in the other,
they were escaping from themselves over the world, in
full view of the world, in a gesture of victory. (249)

Here, then, is sexual pleasure (a *volupté*) distinct from
sexual intimacy. Erik and Riton are "transported," and
this is, one might say, a cultural as well as a sexual
transport. The figurehead, *la figure de proue*, formed
by their bodies projects them out of themselves, out
of any absorption in each other—which is to say out
of the honored tradition that has idealized sexuality
through the image of the intimately conjoined couple.
This quickie on a Paris rooftop thus takes on the value
of a break or seismic shift in a culture's *episteme*: the
injunction to find ourselves, and each other, in the sexual is silenced as, the Nazi and the traitor looking not
at each other but in the same direction, the thrust of
Erik's penis propels him and Riton into the impersonal
Paris night. Our culture tells us to think of sex as the
ultimate privacy, as that intimate knowledge of the other
on which the familial cell is built. Enjoy the rapture
that will never be made public, that will also (though
this is not said) keep you safely, docilely out of the
public realm, that will make you content to allow others to make history while you perfect the oval of a

166
THE GAY OUTLAW

merely copulative or familial intimacy. The sodomist, the public enemy, the traitor, the murderer (Erik and Riton answer to all these titles) are ideally unsuited for such intimacies. Excluded from all triumphant communities (from the heterosexual family to the victorious Allies entering Paris), they are reduced, or elevated, to a kind of objectless or generalized ejaculation, a fucking of the world rather than each other. Because they know they will soon die, this act naturally has some of the desperate and brutal defiance of Genet's "J'encule le monde" (268 in CI), but it also contains—intriguingly for us—the promise of a new kind of fertilization. They come not with each other but, as it were, *to the world,* and in so doing they have the strange but empowering impression of looking at the night as one looks at the future.

For Genet, this "gesture of victory" toward the world depends on an unqualified will to destroy. Not only do Erik and Riton dismiss each other in their lovemaking (they come on the world rather than for each other). Genet's fantasy machine has Riton shoot Erik after sex and then, "all night long, all the morning of August 20, abandoned by his friends, by his parents, by his love, by France, by Germany, by the whole world, he fired away until he fell exhausted," finally to be killed by a French freedom fighter (255). Never has Riton been more faithful to the Nazi cause he so treacherously served than in this final orgy of murderous and suicidal violence.

If there is an ethical hero of historical dimensions in *Funeral Rites*—and we must recognize this as the repellent center of Genet's book—it is Adolf Hitler. Hitler fantasized, to be sure, sexually mythologized and even sexually ridiculed, but close enough to his monstrous real source that we cannot comfortably say that political sympathies are entirely irrelevant to Genet's fantastic scenarios. But it is important to note that neither territorial politics nor any specific genocidal ideology plays a part in Genet's fascination with Nazism. Hitler "destroyed in order to destroy, he killed in order to kill. Nazism sought nothing other than to erect itself proudly in evil, to set up evil as a system and to raise an entire nation, with oneself at the summit of this nation, to the most austere solitude" (not in English; 217 in CI). The Nazism for which Genet professes admiration in his ceremony of treacherous mourning for Jean Decarnin is a myth of absolute betrayal—the betrayal of all human ties, the attempted murder of humanity itself.

Yet this admiration is extremely light in *Funeral Rites*—as if Genet himself recognized how improbable it is. With its casually obscene treatment of Hitler as an old queen, the work could hardly be picked up as an advertisement for Nazism. With its frequent shifts of tone and subject positions (Genet both speaks of Hitler and Erik, for example, in the third person and speaks for them in the first person), *Funeral Rites* is constantly reminding us that identities and convictions cannot be assigned, in fantasy, to particular persons, that the subject responsible for the fantasy cannot be located among the dramatic personae. It is not so much that Genet alternately worships and mocks Hitler, but rather that the *text* is alternately Hitler worshipped and Hitler mocked. But this very irresponsibility, which, however unpleasant, could be appealed to in order to exculpate Genet at least in part for the opinions in *Funeral Rites* (but can fantasies have opinions?), is actually the consummate betrayal in the work, and as such is wholly consonant with the Nazi myth it frivolously treats. The frivolity is Genet's treachery toward the ultimate treachery of Nazism itself. It is a sign of his refusal to enter into any communication whatsoever. Georges Bataille rightly seized upon this refusal as central to Genet's work and, in my view, wrongly condemned him for it. Genet writes without wishing to communicate, thereby depriving his writing of that "ultimate loyalty" without which, for Bataille, no literary work can be "sovereign."[19]

But this is exactly Genet's revolutionary strength. Both his abhorrent glorification of Nazism and his in some ways equally abhorrent failure to take that glorification seriously express his fundamental project of *declining to participate in any sociality at all*. He is, as Bataille also saw, exceptionally cold. But the solitude Genet identifies with evil is undoubtedly unattainable without that gift of coldness. In its celebration of pure destructiveness, *Funeral Rites* seeks to detach evil from its oppositional relation to good, from its dependence on a transgressive mode of address. The work, in its most profound and original resonances, actually makes the very word "evil" obsolete. It would replace the rich social discursiveness of good-and-evil with what might be called the empty value of solitude, a value that literature, always circulating within a symbolic network, can only name. Solitude is evil because it is betrayal, but not a betrayal defined by any opposition to loyalty. It is betrayal of that opposition, a betrayal opposed to nothing because it consists merely in a movement *out* of everything. Nazi murderousness—destruction for the sake of destruction—is, for Genet, the most appropriate historical emblem for this murder of given terms. But to enter into serious "communication" with Nazism would be to misunderstand its mythic importance as a horrific figure for a will to be no longer defined, in good or evil, as human. The Nazism of *Funeral Rites* is not a cause; it is the apocalyptic appearance in history of an impulse to erase history. Pure destruction does not choose its objects; to the extent that all objects are available for relations, there can be no loyalty, no connection, to any object. (Thus, within the Nazi ranks, Riton kills Erik.) In Genet, evil—the ethical corollary of Erik's penile aggression—is an antirelational thrust.

We have yet to address what may be the most intriguing terms in Genet's description of the two men's passionate dismissal of each other. Their positioning in sex is read both as a gesture of victory and as a look into the future. They see nothing in the blanket of night spread over Paris, and yet their gestures of annihilation and their own drop into nothingness are a possible restarting of relational activity. In what way? The scene quickly reminds Genet of Hitler discharging onto his enemies' territory millions of young German males: "It was thus that, from his room in Berlin on Berchtesgaden, Hitler, taking a firm stand, with his stomach striking their backs and his knees in the hollows of theirs, emitted his transfigured adolescents over the humiliated world" (249–250). They are their leader's poisonous seed. Very peculiarly, Genet appears to interpret the renunciation of intimacy implicit in Erik and Riton's sexual positioning as the precondition for an *identity* between the penetrator and the penetrated. Genet simultaneously points his two fantasy figures in the same direction and uncovers a fundamental sameness between them—as if they were relay points in a single burst of erotic energy toward the world. Relationality here takes place only within sameness. This is emphasized in an earlier passage when Hitler-Genet boasts:

> Puny, ridiculous little fellow that I was, I emitted upon the world a power extracted from the pure, sheer beauty of athletes and hoodlums. In the secrecy of my night I took upon myself *(j'endossais)*—the right way of putting it if one bears in mind the homage paid to my body *(à mon dos)*—the beauty of Gérard in particular and then that of all the lads in the Reich: the sailors with a girl's ribbon, the tank crews, the artillerymen, the aces of the Luftwaffe, and the beauty that my love had appropriated was retransmitted by my hands, by my poor puffy, ridiculous face, by my hoarse, [come]-filled mouth to the loveliest armies in the world. Carrying such a charge, which had come from them and returned to them, drunk with themselves and with me, what else could those youngsters do but go out and die? (133)

The men who mount Hitler, and who discharge themselves into him, are themselves penetrated by their own beauty, made drunk by their own jouissance through the medium of a Führer who is indistinguishable from that jouissance. This solipsistic intensification of sexual energy—the production of the soldier's orgasm by his own (retransmitted) orgasm—"completes" the Nazi murder of humanity with a suicidal self-replication in the murderous subject. And yet this absolute narcissism also opens a path onto the world, a world emptied of relations but where relationality has to be reinvented if the dangerously overloaded self is to escape the fatally orgasmic implosions of Hitler's soldiers. (The successful blockage of energy within a perfectly realized and definitive homo-ness is incompatible with life.[20]) The future that Riton and Erik appear to be looking at must somehow emerge from the radical homo-ness of their homosexual adventure, from their refusal, or inability, to love anything *other* than themselves—which might be translated politically as their failure to accept a relation with any given social arrangement.

This is not a political program. Just as Genet's fascination with what he outrageously calls the beauty of Nazism is in no way a plea for the specific goals pursued by Nazi Germany, Erik and Riton are positioned for a reinventing of the social without any indication about how such a reinvention might proceed historically or what face it might have. *Funeral Rites* does nothing more—but I think it's a great deal—than propose the fantasmatic conditions of possibility for such a proceeding. It insists on the continuity between the sexual and the political, and while this superficially glorifies Nazism as the system most congenial to a cult of male power justified by little more than male beauty, it also transforms the historical reality of Nazism into a mythic metaphor for a revolutionary destructiveness which would surely dissolve the rigidly defined sociality of Nazism itself. Still, the metaphoric suitability of Hitler's regime for this project can hardly be untroubling.

It reminds us only too clearly that Genet's political radicalism is congruent with a proclaimed indifference to human life as well as a willingness to betray every tie and every trust between human beings. This is the evil that becomes Genet's good, and, as if that were not sufficiently noxious, homosexuality is enlisted as the prototype of relations that break with humanity, that elevate infecundity, waste, and sameness to requirements for the production of pleasure.

There may be only one reason to tolerate, even to welcome, *Funeral Rites*'s rejection (at once exasperated and clownish) of relationality: without such a rejection, social revolt is doomed to repeat the oppressive conditions that provoked the revolt. This argument is strongly implied in Genet's early play *The Maids*. In his prefatory comments on how *The Maids* should be performed, Genet dismisses any view of his play (which should, he says, be acted nonrealistically) as a plea on behalf of maids. "I suppose," he adds, "that there is a union for domestic servants—that's not our affair."[21] Perhaps not—but Solange, defying Madame through her sister Claire playing the role of Madame, mocks her mistress' illusion that she was "protected by her barricade of flowers, saved by some special destiny, by a sacrifice. But she reckoned without a maid's rebellion. Behold her wrath, Madame *(C'était compter sans la révolte des bonnes. La voice qui monte, Madame)*."[22] There is, then, a rebellion in *The Maids*, one more real than any revolt that might be realistically conceived. The condition of domestics is merely a social problem; what interests Genet is not how society distributes predicaments, but rather how it assigns identities. It is the taking on—or attempted refusal—of those identities that determines effective rebellion.

In a sense, Genet is an out-and-out social constructionist. There is no margin of being to which Claire and Solange can retreat, no secret inner place their social nature couldn't reach or violate, and which might reconcile them to being maids. In *The Maids,* social roles are inner essences, and the question becomes: how do you get rid of an essence (or as a *pis aller,* change essences)? Interestingly, Genet answers this question through an intricate play with relationships. The essence is indeed like a frozen block of being, but it has only a relational existence. Maidness is the relation between Madame and the two maids, as well as between the maids. What and how a maid "is" is entirely spelled out within the cultural construction of those relations. It includes not only being submissive to Madame, being in awe of her, idolizing and envying her beauty and wealth, but also resenting her, willing her death. The maids' dilemma is that there is nothing they might do to Madame that would not confirm their identity as maids. Even to kill her—though it is not an intrinsic part of the social scenario within which they are inscribed—would transgress their maid-subjectivity in a way determined by that scenario. Transgressiveness is part of their identity. Furthermore, it is far from certain that killing Madame would liberate them from their disgust with each other or from their imitation of their relation to Madame. Before Madame's return home, Claire taunts Solange by telling her that she, unlike Solange (who couldn't strangle the sleeping Madame), will have the courage to kill Madame by serving her poisoned tea, and she adds:

"It's my turn now to dominate you!" (61;59). Their fate—and it has been the fate of more than one revolutionary movement—may be to repeat, after they have freed themselves from Madame, the very structure of oppression that led to their revolt. Revolt allows for new agents to fill the slots of master and slave, but it does not necessarily include a new imagining of how to structure human relations. Structures of oppression outlive agents of oppression.

The Maids does, however, suggest a mutation in the structure itself. Claire admits to Solange that as their habitual "ceremony" approaches its climax, she always protects her own neck, for "through her, it was me you were aiming at. I'm the one who's in danger" (55;48). Given the self-hatred (and the adulation of Madame) inscribed in their essence, this is normal enough. But in the final moments of the play, this potential violence is radically resignified, and in a way that ejects them from the field of resignification. Just before Claire, as Madame, insists that Solange give her the poisoned tea, Solange has a long monologue in which she imagines killing Claire for the latter's failure, a few minutes earlier, to make Madame take the poisoned drink. She gets excited at the idea of leaping into a new role ("I'm the strangler. Mademoiselle Solange, the one who strangled her sister!"), with a new title: "Now we are Mademoiselle Lemercier, that Lemercier woman. The famous criminal" (93–95;107–109). But this exhausts her and, ending the game, she tells Claire that they are finished, lost. Claire has been listening, however, and now insists that Solange really kill her (Solange, having returned to "reality," at first resists), but with a differ-

ence: not as her sister, but as Madame. This would
seem to bring them back to the familiar scenario we
saw at the beginning of the play. But then they were
rehearsing for the murder of Madame. In despair, Solange, as we have just seen, also imagines killing Claire.
In this dialectical progression, the third and final step
at once transcends, reconciles, and erases the first two:
Madame will be killed in play, but the play killing her
will be the murder of Claire. Step three contains steps
one and two, and neither one of them: it would be
wrong to say that they have really murdered Madame,
just as it would be wrong to say that Solange has deliberately done away with her sister. She hands the
poisoned drink to "Madame," and it is Claire who will
be poisoned. There is a real death that is doubly de-re-
alized: Madame survives (since it is Claire who is poisoned), but Claire also survives since it is she who gives
the drink to Claire-as-Madame.

Only now can we appreciate the profound rightness
of a superficially unnecessary aspect of the original ceremony: Solange becomes Claire when the latter takes on
the role of Madame. This moving outside herself allows Claire to survive her own death. Before drinking
the tea that she will drink as Madame, Claire reminds
Solange twice that she, Claire, will now be living in
Solange: "Solange, you will contain me within you,"
and "It will be your task, yours alone, to keep us both
alive . . . In prison no one will know that I'm with you,
secretly. On the sly" (96–97).[23] No one will know. Solange will be condemned for killing her sister, whereas
both she and Claire know that she has "really" killed
Madame. The play's climax enacts their new knowl-

edge that the only effective way of getting rid of Madame is through the ceremony. The problem has been all along how they might murder Madame without merely fulfilling their destiny as servile and rebellious maids. The answer, they discover, is to eliminate her as a relational term, and this can be done only if Claire's death is misinterpreted by others. Society, which has locked them into their maidness, will also liberate them by not seeing Madame's place in the murder. And I should emphasize that they have not simply switched essences—which is what Solange has in mind when she anticipates being reviled as "the strangler" or when, remembering her wish to set the house on fire after killing Madame, she refers to "Incendiary!" as a "splendid title" (57;51). The social world of essences has been replaced by a private domain of fractured and multiple identities.

Because no one will know that Solange is harboring Claire within her, or that Claire was addressing Solange as Claire when she asked for the poisoned tea, or that Claire was impersonating Madame when she drank it, we could also say: it doesn't matter, since nothing has changed in the world. But nothing *can* change in this world—or rather (and this, it must be acknowledged, is an uncertain bet), between oppression now and freedom later there may have to be a radical break with the social itself. What could be stranger? In this play, which, Genet insists, must not be taken realistically and which, within its unreality, does distinguish between the maids' ceremony and their real lives, it is the unreal within the unreal that carries the heaviest social and political burden. The maids' revolt (and the revolt of all the oppressed?) will be effective only if their subjectivity can no longer be related to as an oppressed subjectivity. Madame may attend Solange's trial, but she has nonetheless been killed as that difference from the maids that constituted them as maids. Once more, it is perhaps Genet's homosexuality that allowed him to imagine a curative collapsing of social difference into a radical homo-ness, where the subject might begin again, differentiating itself from itself and thereby reconstituting sociality.

Nothing could be more antagonistic to monumental art than this project. *Funeral Rites* in particular is a battle between two aesthetics. On the one hand, Genet promotes, and has been most easily recognized by, a notion of art as the cultivation of gestural beauty. This is art as a defiant display of a self perfected in its gestures, as a kind of antidialogic address to its audience. This gestural self, Genet seems to hope, might even outlive the phenomenal self that originally produced the gesture. Like Erik, who "desired his own realization," Genet aspires to see himself complete *(achevé)* even if only for one day (119). Wholly "realized," a fully finished artifact, Genet can die, assured of the eerie immortality of a beautiful pose detached from both its source and its audience.

On the other hand, Genet mistrusts beauty. It transforms a formula into "a closed thing, a thing in itself"; the showiness or eclat of "brilliant expressions" arrests the mind, and those expressions become a "prison for the mind that embellishes them and refuses to escape" (not in English; 187 in CI). This prison is also that of the self in solitude at the end of its ascetic pilgrim's progress toward evil, with difference now reduced to intervallic sameness. (The soldiers buggering Hitler, Hitler himself, and the soldiers on the battlefield spatially distribute a single sexual energy; Claire *is* Solange, but at a certain inner distance from Solange's consciousness of their sameness.) How can art indicate a way out of such a prison?

Once again we must turn to Genet's cherished activity of rimming, which turns out to be just as suggestive aesthetically as it is ethically. Not only do Genet's murderous fantasies as he rims Jean consummate their union as undifferentiated waste. Genet also resurrects a world as his tongue drills into his lover's anus:

> Then I tried hard to do as good a job as a drill. As the workman in the quarry leans on his machine that jolts him amidst splinters of mica and sparks from his drill, a merciless sun beats down on the back of his neck, and a sudden dizziness blurs everything and sets out the usual palm trees and springs of a mirage, in like manner a dizziness shook my prick harder, my tongue grew soft, forgetting to dig harder, my head sank deeper into the damp hairs, and I saw the eye of Gabès [the anus] become adorned with flowers, with foliage, become a cool bower which I crawled to and entered with my entire body, to sleep on the moss there, in the shade, to die there. (253)

Even if Genet himself disappears (dies) during such a vision, a world is getting born. The rimmer in his jouissance has demiurgic powers. Genet is orally impregnated by eating his lover's waste. Having eaten Jean as death, Genet expels him as a world of new images. There is, to be sure, a reversal of given terms here: the anus produces life, waste is fecund, from death new landscapes emerge. But perhaps such reversals could take place only after the entire field of resignifying potentialities has been devastated. With relationality eliminated, values can be remembered posthumously and reversed without the risk of contaminating the reversal by the old terms.[24]

This is Genet's ingenious solution to the problem of revolutionary beginnings condemned to repeat old orders: he dies so that repetition itself may become an initiating act. This can be accomplished only if dying is conceived, and experienced, as jouissance. The fertility of rimming depends on its being immediately productive. The hallucinatory excitement induced in Genet by his foraging tongue gives birth at once to the luxuriant bouquets and bowers of his writing. Not only does this type of sublimation bypass the social as a field of symbolic substitutions for the sexual; it is not even the result of that "cathexis of ego tendencies" by a free-floating sexual energy, detached from specific desires, which Melanie Klein equated with "the capacity to sublimate."[25] Instead, sublimation here is an activity of consciousness accompanying a particular sexual activity, indeed lasting no longer than that activity. The symbolic is a product of the body, and it is a by no means insignificant element of Genet's subversiveness that he performatively refutes the reactionary Lacanian doctrine that instructs us to think of language as castration, as cutting us off from the revolutionary potential of the body.

Of course Genet's visions are textual fragments; they have none of the closed monumentality of beauty's perfected gestures. Not only that; they are disposable. "The poet," Genet writes in *Funeral Rites*, "is interested in error since only error teaches truth . . . Poetry or the art of using remains *(La poésie ou l'art d'utiliser les restes)*. These errors may serve, or be, the beauty of the future" (not in English; 190 in CI). In a society where oppression is structural, constitutive of sociality itself, only what that society throws off—its mistakes or its pariahs—can serve the future. In Genet, error is the aesthetic and social equivalent of fecal matter; it has all the paradoxical promise of fertility and renewal that Genet associates with waste. But as the waste of the mind, error also has the immense advantage of being expendable. Perhaps we won't need it; perhaps it won't serve. "This book," Genet says of *Funeral Rites,* "is sincere and it's a joke."[26] Just as the radical lightness mentioned earlier counters Genet's seriousness about Nazism (even as his betrayal of that seriousness is consistent with the massive betrayal of humanity itself in Nazism), so he is willing to be unfaithful to his own work. The humor in *Funeral Rites* is the tonal sign of Genet's refusal to establish a certain kind of communication—culturally consecrated—between the author and his work. He will not be entirely serious about literature.

To have Genet's authorization to think of *Funeral Rites* as expendable can be a relief: it makes us less troubled by the author's fascination with betrayal, murder, and death. But Genet's partial dismissal of his work is itself culturally threatening. It betrays the ethic of seriousness that governs our usual relation to art, inviting us to view literature, for example, not as epistemological and moral monuments but, possibly, as cultural droppings. In this, Genet is much like Beckett who, in his determination to fail, would have to be in sympathy with Genet's scatological aesthetic. The cult of failure and the cult of waste: Beckett and Genet belong to a radical modernity anxious to save art from the preemptive operations of institutionalized culture. They defy us to take them seriously, they won't let us believe that they have been successful artists or told us some important truths. But they do, finally, let us hear them failing or getting high on linguistic waste, and so they compel us, perhaps in spite of themselves, to rethink what we mean and what we expect from communication, and from community.

Notes

Index

Notes

Prologue

1. Monique Wittig, *The Straight Mind and Other Essays* (Boston: Beacon Press, 1992), p. 32. Judith Butler, "Imitation and Gender Insubordination," in *Inside/Out: Lesbian Theories, Gay Theories*, ed. Diana Fuss (New York: Routledge, 1991), p. 17. Michael Warner, introduction to *Fear of a Queer Planet: Queer Politics and Social Theory*, ed. Warner (Minneapolis: University of Minnesota Press, 1993), p. xxvi.
2. Michael Warner, "Thoreau's Bottom," *Raritan*, 11 (Winter 1992), 65.
3. Steven Seidman, "Identity and Politics in a 'Postmodern' Gay Culture," in *Fear of a Queer Planet*, p. 137.
4. Warner, *Fear of a Queer Planet*, p. xv.
5. Leo Bersani, "Is the Rectum a Grave?" in *AIDS: Cultural Analysis, Cultural Activism*, ed. Douglas Crimp (Cambridge: MIT Press, 1988), p. 206.

1. *The Gay Presence*

1. Andrew Kopkind, "The Gay Moment," *Nation,* 256 (May 3, 1993), 590–602.
2. Jane Gross, "Gay Sailor's Colleagues Remain Upset," *New York Times,* April 3, 1993, section A, p. 12.
3. D. A. Miller, *Bringing Out Roland Barthes* (Berkeley: University of California Press, 1992), p. 31.
4. Jacques Lacan, "The Signification of the Phallus," *Ecrits: A Selection,* tr. Alan Sheridan (New York: Norton, 1977), p. 291.
5. National Research Council, *The Social Impact of AIDS in the United States,* ed. Albert R. Jonsen and Jeff Stryker (Washington, D.C.: National Academy Press, 1993), pp. 7–9.
6. Ibid., p. 65. I should add that "objectivity" also leads the council to conclude: "Perhaps the most profound impact of AIDS on health care has been a renewed appreciation of, and heightened attention to, the risk of blood-borne pathogens" (p. 72). What does "profound" mean in the conclusion of a largely statistical survey, and, more important, what does this "impact" suggest about American health care? The council never pushed this far.
7. Ibid., pp. 9, 273–275.

2. *The Gay Absence*

1. Mary McIntosh, "The Homosexual Role" (1968), reprinted in *Forms of Desire: Sexual Orientation and the Social Constructionist Controversy,* ed. Edward Stein (New York: Routledge, 1992), p. 27.
2. Steven Epstein, "Gay Politics, Ethnic Identity: The Limits of Social Constructionism," in *Forms of Desire,* p. 252.
3. Dennis Altman, *Homosexual: Oppression and Liberation* (New York: Outerbridge, 1971).

4. Epstein, "Gay Politics," p. 254.

5. Michel Foucault, *The History of Sexuality,* vol. 1, *An Introduction,* tr. Robert Hurley (New York: Vintage, 1978, 1990), p. 101.

6. Ibid., p. 43. John Boswell persuasively argues that while "ancient and medieval sexual constructs were unrelated to the modern differentiation between homosexual and heterosexual 'orientation,' 'identity,' or 'preference,'" this does not mean that earlier societies failed to recognize lifelong homosexual or heterosexual commitment. Boswell, "Categories, Experience and Sexuality," *Forms of Desire,* p. 172.

7. Edward Stein, "Conclusion: The Essentials of Constructionism and the Construction of Essentialism," *Forms of Desire,* p. 340.

8. Lee Edelman, *Homographesis: Essays in Gay Literary and Cultural Theory* (New York: Routledge, 1994), p. 39. In an analysis of the 1944 film *Laura* in this same volume (and especially of the function of the Clifton Webb character, Waldo), Edelman speaks of the gay man as "both *necessary* to confirm the 'integrity' of the face of male heterosexuality and *intolerable* in so far as his presence is a reminder of the fictionality of that face" (p. 238). Further, in a stunning essay on Alfred Hitchcock's *Rope,* D. A. Miller argues for the "social utility" of castration anxiety in maintaining a heterosexual male identity. Far from being the anxiety-ridden property of the woman and the homosexual, castration may be *needed* in order to generate, in the straight man, the fear and the comfort that keep him securely straight. *Rope* raises the frightening possibility that being fucked does *not* entail castration (so that "homosexuality would be characterized not by a problematics of castration, but on the contrary by an exemption from one"). More terrifying than the fear of castration is the "oddly compatible fear of the nega-

tion of castration." Miller, "Anal *Rope,*" in *Inside/Out: Lesbian Theories, Gay Theories,* ed. Diana Fuss (New York: Routledge, 1991), pp. 135–38.

9. As Kenneth Lewes writes, "It is not accurate to speak of 'normal' or 'natural' development in the case of the Oedipus complex, since these terms suggest an orderly efflorescence of possibilities inherent in the individual before he enters the oedipal stage. The mechanisms of the Oedipus complex are really a series of psychic traumas, and all results of it are neurotic compromise formations. Since even optimal development is the result of trauma, the fact that a certain development results from a 'stunting' or 'blocking' or 'inhibition' of another possibility does not distinguish it from other developments. So all results of the Oedipus complex are traumatic, and, for similar reasons, all are 'normal.'" Lewes, *The Psychoanalytic Theory of Male Homosexuality* (New York: New American Library, 1988), p. 82. See also the essay by John Fletcher, "Freud and His Uses: Psychoanalysis and Gay Theory," in *Coming On Strong: Gay Politics and Culture,* ed. Simon Shepherd and Mick Wallis (London: Unwin Hyman, 1989).

10. Judith Butler, *Gender Trouble: Feminism and the Subversion of Identity* (New York: Routledge, 1990), pp. 60–61.

11. Jonathan Dollimore makes an argument for the perverse "not as a unitary, pre-social libido, or an original plenitude, but as a transgressive agency inseparable from a dynamic intrinsic to social process." This dynamic "generates instabilities within repressive norms." Dollimore, *Sexual Dissidence: Augustine to Wilde, Freud to Foucault* (Oxford: Clarendon Press, 1991), p. 33.

12. Michael Warner, "Homo-Narcissism; or, Heterosexuality," in *Engendering Men: The Question of Male Femi-*

nist Criticism, ed. Joseph A. Boone and Michael Cadden (New York: Routledge, 1990), p. 200.

13. Bonnie B. Spanier, "'Lessons' From 'Nature': Gender Ideology and Sexual Ambiguity in Biology," in *Body Guards: The Cultural Politics of Gender Ambiguity,* ed. Julia Epstein and Kristina Straub (New York: Routledge, 1991), pp. 334, 336.

14. Monique Wittig, *The Straight Mind and Other Essays* (Boston: Beacon Press, 1992), pp. 42–43.

15. Ibid., p. 29.

16. Lewes, *Psychoanalytic Theory of Male Homosexuality,* p. 80.

17. Wittig, *Straight Mind,* pp. 5, 13, 32.

18. Butler, *Gender Trouble,* pp. 120–121.

19. "Gender is an ontological impossibility because it tries to accomplish the division of Being. But Being as being is not divided." Wittig, *Straight Mind,* p. 81.

20. Butler, *Gender Trouble,* p. 114.

21. Ibid., pp. 5, 109–110, 132.

22. Ibid., pp. 121–22, 137, 124.

23. Ibid., p. 122.

24. Butler, *Bodies That Matter: On the Discursive Limits of "Sex"* (New York: Routledge, 1993), p. 94.

25. Butler, "Critically Queer," *GLQ: A Journal of Lesbian and Gay Studies,* 1.1 (1993), 21.

26. Butler, *Bodies That Matter,* p. 125. In a provocative review of *Paris Is Burning,* bell hooks has criticized the "imperial overseeing position" adopted by the filmmaker Livingston. See "Is Paris Burning," *Z,* Sisters of the Yam column (June 1991).

27. Butler, *Bodies That Matter,* p. 137.

28. Adrienne Rich, "Compulsory Heterosexuality and Lesbian Existence," in *Powers of Desire: The Politics of Sexuality,* ed. Ann Snitow, Christine Stansell, and Sharon

Thompson (New York: Monthly Review Press, 1983), pp. 191–193.

29. A citation from Jeffreys' 1985 book, *The Spinster and Her Enemies: Feminism and Sexuality, 1880–1930,* quoted in Margaret Hunt, "Report of a Conference on Feminism, Sexuality and Power: The Elect Clash with the Perverse," in *Coming to Power: Writings and Graphics on Lesbian S/M,* ed. SAMOIS, a lesbian-feminist organization (Boston: Alyson Publications, 1981, 1982, 1987), p. 88.

30. Amber Hollibaugh and Cherríe Moraga, "What We're Rollin' Around in Bed With: Sexual Silences in Feminism," *Powers of Desire,* p. 396, and Gayle Rubin, "The Leather Menace: Comments on Politics and S/M," *Coming to Power,* p. 214.

31. David M. Halperin, *One Hundred Years of Homosexuality and Other Essays on Greek Love* (New York: Routledge, 1990), p. 26.

32. Butler, "Imitation and Gender Insubordination," *Inside/Out,* p. 17.

33. Eve Kosofsky Sedgwick, *Epistemology of the Closet* (Berkeley: University of California Press, 1990), p. 41.

34. Halperin, *One Hundred Years of Homosexuality,* p. 49.

35. Sedgwick, *Epistemology of the Closet,* pp. 40–41.

36. See the interesting exchange on the topic of gay genes, "Evidence for Queer Genes: An Interview with Richard Pillard," interview and commentary by Edward Stein, *GLQ,* 1.1 (1993), 93–110. Pillard has published, with Michael Barley, a study of sexual orientation and twins which concludes that gay genes are real: "A Genetic Study of Male Sexual Orientation," *Archives of General Psychiatry,* 48 (1991), 1089–96.

37. Perhaps because of this avoidance, Richard Mohr not only argues that "the time has come for gay intellectuals to stop being afraid of nature—both the concept and the

thing," but also speaks favorably of "male separatism"—
of a kind of new priesthood whose St. Peter might be
Tom of Finland (the gay artist known for his massive
and massively endowed male figures having what is often
fabulously improbable sex). "Hypermasculine interac-
tions hold out the possibility of serving as models of
equality," of that "mutual respect on which all other
values of democracy depend." Mohr's case is a refresh-
ing antidote to some of the ethereal abstractions I've
been referring to, but for me the appeal of its raunchi-
ness is considerably diminished by the banalizing respectability it takes on when yoked to equality, democracy, and the priesthood. Mohr, *Gay Ideas: Outing and
Other Controversies* (Boston: Beacon Press, 1992), pp. 7,
173, 195.

38. See Kaja Silverman, *Male Subjectivity at the Margins,*
(New York: Routledge, 1992). For an original and valuable attempt to elaborate a lesbian specificity grounded
in lesbian sexuality, see Teresa de Lauretis, *The Practice
of Love* (Bloomington: Indiana University Press, 1994).

39. In her most recent work Judith Butler has, very interestingly, been redefining citationality in terms of "cross-
ings-over" in fantasmatic identifications. "Identifications
that cross gender boundaries can reinstitute sexed bodies in variable ways." Butler, *Bodies That Matter,* p. 91.

40. Henry Louis Gates Jr., "Backlash?" *New Yorker,* 49 (May
17, 1993), 42–44.

41. See Gloria Anzaldúa, *Borderlands: La Frontera* (San
Francisco: Spinsters/Aunt Lute, 1987).

42. Bersani, "Is the Rectum a Grave?" in *AIDS: Cultural
Analysis, Cultural Activism,* ed. Douglas Crimp (Cambridge: MIT Press, 1988), p. 206.

43. These unions are generally thought of as disrupting sexual classification, as saving erotic desire from the neat

categorical opposition between hetero- and homosexuality. See Pat Califia, "Gay Men, Lesbians, and Sex: Doing It Together," *Advocate*, July 7, 1983, pp. 24–27; Gorjet Harper, "Lesbians Who Sleep with Men," *Outweek*, February 11, 1990, pp. 46–52.

44. Boone and Cadden, *Engendering Men*, pp. 1–2.

45. Sedgwick, *Epistemology of the Closet*, p. 1.

46. Edelman, *Homographesis*, pp. xiv–xv.

47. Tony Kushner, *Angels in America: A Gay Fantasia on National Themes*, 1: *Millennium Approaches* (New York: Theatre Communications Group, 1992), p. 72.

48. Tania Modleski, *Feminism Without Women: Culture and Criticism in a "Postfeminist" Age* (New York: Routledge, 1991), pp. 69–70. See also *Men in Feminism*, ed. Alice Jardine and Paul Smith (New York: Routledge, 1987).

49. See Michael Warner, ed., *Fear of a Queer Planet: Queer Politics and Social Theory* (Minneapolis: University of Minnesota Press, 1993). There is already an impressive bibliography in queer theory, although much of what passes for queer could just as easily have been called gay—if, that is, there hadn't been a change in lexical fashion. Several of the essays in Warner's important collection have the advantage of seriously pursuing a persuasive specificity in the concept of queer. "Queer" would certainly include gays, but its theorists reject the notion of a universally valid gay identity. Identities are historically variable; they are provisionally defined by, among other things, ethnic and class particularities. For other essays that put themselves in the queer category, see the issue of *differences* devoted to "Queer Theory: Lesbian and Gay Sexualities," 3 (Summer 1991). For discussions of the term, see the interviews and articles in the special section of *Out/Look: National Lesbian and Gay Quarterly*, 11 (Winter 1991). In this issue Jeffrey Escoffier and

Allan Bérubé write: "*Queer* is meant to be confrontational—opposed to gay assimilationists and straight oppressors while inclusive of people who have been marginalized by anyone in power" (p. 14). Also useful are essays by Lisa Duggan, "Making It Perfectly Queer," and by Arlene Stein, "Sisters and Queers," in *Socialist Review,* 22.1 (1992). For Duggan, this new queer community "is unified only by a shared dissent from the dominant organization of sex and gender" (p. 20). Eve Kosofsky Sedgwick's work has exercised considerable influence on the development of queer theory. See her *Tendencies* (Durham: Duke University Press, 1993).

50. Steven Seidman, "Identity and Politics in a 'Postmodern' Gay Culture," *Fear of a Queer Planet,* p. 136.

51. Warner, ibid., p. xiii.

52. Warner, "Thoreau's Bottom," *Raritan,* 11 (Winter 1992), p. 78.

53. Cindy Patton, "Tremble, Hetero Swine!," *Fear of a Queer Planet,* pp. 147–148.

54. Lauren Berlant and Elizabeth Freeman, "Queer Nationality," ibid., pp. 196, 212, 221.

55. Warner, ibid., pp. xxv, xxvii.

3. *The Gay Daddy*

1. Michel Foucault, interview with James O'Higgins, *Salmagundi,* 58–59 (Fall 1982–Winter 1983), 10–24; reprinted as "Sexual Choice, Sexual Act: Foucault and Homosexuality," in *Michel Foucault: Politics, Philosophy, Culture, Interviews and Other Writings, 1977–1984,* ed. Lawrence D. Kritzman (New York: Routledge, 1988), p. 301.

2. "Michel Foucault, le gai savoir," interview with Jean Le Bitoux, *Mec,* 5 (June 1988), 35. My translation.

3. Ibid., p. 35.
4. "Michel Foucault: Sex, Power, and the Politics of Identity," interview with Bob Gallagher and Alexander Wilson, *Advocate*, 400 (August 7, 1984), 27.
5. Interview with O'Higgins, *Foucault*, p. 300.
6. Foucault, *The History of Sexuality*, vol. 1, tr. Robert Hurley (New York: Vintage, 1990), p. 93.
7. Introduction, *S and M: Studies in Sadomasochism*, ed. Thomas Weinberg and G. W. Levi Kamel (Buffalo: Prometheus Books, 1983), p. 21.
8. Geoff Mains, *Urban Aboriginals: A Celebration of Leathersexuality* (San Francisco: Gay Sunshine Press, 1984), p. 83.
9. Robert H. Hopcke, "S/M and the Psychology of Male Initiation: An Archetypal Perspective," in *Leatherfolk: Radical Sex, People, Politics and Practice*, ed. Mark Thompson (Boston: Alyson Publications, 1991), p. 74.
10. Thompson, *Leatherfolk*, p. xvii.
11. Mains, *Urban Aboriginals*, p. 73.
12. Thompson, *Leatherfolk*, p. xii.
13. Mains, *Urban Aboriginals*, p. 73.
14. Pat Califia, "A Secret Side of Lesbian Sexuality," *S and M*, p. 135.
15. Michael Bronski, "A Dream Is a Wish Your Heart Makes: Notes on the Materialization of Sexual Fantasy," *Leatherfolk*, p. 64.
16. Hopke, "S/M," p. 71. According to Parveen Adams, only the lesbian sadomasochist avoids this bond to the paternal phallus and the oedipal law. Lesbian S/M "appears not to be compulsive, can just as easily be genital or not, and is an affair of women." It is a practice of "mobility," "consent," and "satisfaction." Adams, "Of Female Bondage," in *Between Feminism and Psychoanalysis*, ed. Teresa Brennan (New York: Routledge, 1989), pp. 262–263.

17. Califia, "Secret Side," p. 135.

18. Foucault, "Sade, sergent du sexe," *Cinématographe,* 16 (1975), 5.

19. Foucault, interview in *Advocate,* p. 30.

20. Foucault, in "Sade," p. 5.

21. Juicy Lucy, "If I Ask You to Tie Me Up, Will You Still Want to Love Me?" in *Coming to Power: Writings and Graphics on Lesbian S/M,* ed. SAMOIS (Boston: Alyson Publications, 1981), pp. 31, 35. Others have noted this dismissal of torture in sympathetic discussions of S/M. Mandy Merck writes that while "a few cruelties may be alluded to" in these discussions, "the subjectivity which enacts them is never examined," and Tania Modleski points out that the emphasis on consensuality in S/M "has meant a neglect of some of the most important, indeed the defining, features of S/M—the infliction of pain and humiliation by one individual on another—features requiring explanation even if they *are* desired by all parties." Merck, *Perversion: Deviant Readings* (New York: Routledge, 1993), p. 256; Modleski, *Feminism Without Women* (New York: Routledge, 1991), p. 154.

22. John Preston, "What Happened?", *Leatherfolk,* p. 219.

23. Mains, *Urban Aboriginals,* p. 59; Mains, "Molecular Anatomy of Leather," *Leatherfolk,* p. 41.

24. Juicy Lucy, "If I Ask You," p. 33.

25. The Deleuzian separation of masochism from sadism politically sentimentalizes masochism as a resistance to power, thus bypassing the excitement of submitting to power (whether exercised by a man or a woman). By eliminating the sadistic subject from the masochistic scenario, Deleuze's analysis (in *Masochism: An Interpretation of Coldness and Cruelty*) blinds us to sadistic power's most profound appeal (and so to its ineradicability): the promise it contains of masochistic surrender. In

Modleski's version of lesbian S/M, which is close to the Deleuzian model, the woman in the position of power "serves an almost archetypal function, initiating the woman into symbolic order, but transferring and transforming a patriarchal system of gender inequities into a realm of difference presided over by women." She acknowledges that the "complex dynamic" enacted by lesbian S/M simultaneously contests and preserves "existing gender arrangements" (*Feminism Without Women,* pp. 156–157). A question to consider: does the absence of a man in a S/M relation change the function of power worship as radically as Modleski and, for different reasons, Parveen Adams maintain? Since the kick, the jouissance, of S/M depends both on the exercise and on the relinquishing of power, the gender of the participants seems to me irrelevant to S/M's reinforcement of prevailing structures of domination and oppression. Lesbian S/M may contest the most frequent gender arrangements within those structures, but the rule of the Law (whether presided over by a man or a woman) can hardly be "derided" (as Deleuze argues) as long as that rule continues to be experienced as thrilling (that is, as long as S/M is practiced and other, less oppressive ways of exploiting the eroticism inherent in power have not been explored).

26. *Three Essays on the Theory of Sexuality* (1905), in *The Standard Edition of the Complete Psychological Works of Sigmund Freud,* ed. James Strachey, 24 vols. (London: Hogarth Press, 1953–1974), 7:184.

27. Foucault, interview in *Mec,* p. 34. My translation.

28. David M. Halperin, *One Hundred Years of Homosexuality and Other Essays on Greek Love* (New York: Routledge, 1990), pp. 32, 25, 30.

29. Freud, "From the History of an Infantile Neurosis" ([1914] 1918), in *Standard Edition,* 17: 45, 66, 86, 67.

30. Ibid., pp. 88, 86.
31. Ibid., p. 101.

4. *The Gay Outlaw*

1. André Gide, *The Immoralist*, tr. Richard Howard (New York: Vintage, 1970), p. 3. Subsequent page references to this edition will be given in the text.
2. An important exception is Michael Lucey, whose book, *Gide's Bent: Writing, Sexuality, Politics* (New York: Oxford University Press, forthcoming), should make impossible any such reticence in future discussions of Gide.
3. John Berger, *Keeping a Rendezvous* (New York: Pantheon, 1991), p. 167.
4. Marcel Proust, *Cities of the Plain* (English title for *Sodome et Gomorrhe*), in *Remembrance of Things Past*, tr. C. K. Scott Moncrieff and Terence Kilmartin, 3 vols. (New York: Vintage, 1982), 2:638–639. Subsequent page references to Proust will be given in the text; unless otherwise indicated, they are all from vol. 2.
5. Michel Foucault, *The History of Sexuality*, vol. 1 (New York: Vintage, 1990), p. 43.
6. Proust, *Le Carnet de 1908*, ed. Philip Kolb (Paris: Gallimard, 1976), p. 63. Antoine Compagnon quotes this passage in his commentary on *Sodome et Gomorrhe* in Proust, *A la Recherche du temps perdu*, vol. 3 (Paris: Gallimard, 1988), p. 1270. Compagnon rightly points out that Proust conceives of inversion "not as that of the desired object, but rather that of the desiring subject" (p. 1217).
7. I assume a symmetry between lesbianism and male homosexuality, a symmetry that the text may seem logically to require but that in fact, as Eve Kosofsky Sedgwick points out, the narrator fails to establish. See her

chapter on Proust in *Epistemology of the Closet* (Berkeley: University of California Press, 1990).

8. Freud, *The Interpretation of Dreams,* in *Standard Edition,* 5:567.

9. Kaja Silverman, *Male Subjectivity at the Margins* (New York: Routledge, 1992), esp. pp. 264ff.

10. Sedgwick, *Epistemology of the Closet,* p. 220.

11. As Diana Fuss has pointed out, Freud identifies homosexuality with a lack of lack (although this also means, for Freud, that there can be no homosexual desire): "For Freud, homosexual desire is oxymoronic; like women, homosexuals (male and female) lack lack, or lack a certain mature relation to lack. By temporally positing homosexuality as antecedent to the lack that inaugurates desire, Freud in effect drops the sexuality out of homosexuality. It is not lack that defines a homo(sexual) subject but excess, the lack of lack." Fuss, "Freud's Fallen Women: Identification, Desire, and 'A Case of Homosexuality in a Woman,'" in *Fear of a Queer Planet,* ed. Michael Warner (Minneapolis: University of Minnesota Press, 1993), pp. 55–56.

12. In Paul Morrison's formulation of the panoptic nature of the psychologizing of relations: "Love is the heterosexual policing of desire." See his "End Pleasure," *GLQ,* 1.1 (1993), 71.

13. Edmund White, introduction to Jean Genet, *Prisoner of Love,* tr. Barbara Bray (Middletown: Wesleyan University Press, 1992), p. xiii.

14. Jean Genet, *Funeral Rites,* tr. Bernard Frechtman (New York: Grove Press, 1969), p. 80. Subsequent page references to this edition will be given in the text. In the 1953 edition of *Pompes funèbres* published by Gallimard as part of the *Oeuvres complètes,* several passages from the original version (also published in 1953 as a separate

volume in the Gallimard Collection Imaginaire) are omitted. Frechtman's translation follows the version from the *Oeuvres complètes*. I have translated and indicated the few passages I use from the original text (CI) that are not in his version.

My thinking about Genet has been stimulated by discussions in a graduate seminar at Berkeley in the fall of 1993, and in particular by the contributions of Gitanjali Kapila and Leslie Minot.

15. Judith Butler, "Critically Queer," *GLQ*, 1.1 (1993), esp. 23, 26.

16. This is a principal thesis in Jean-Paul Sartre, *Genet: Actor and Martyr*, tr. Bernard Frechtman (New York: Braziller, 1963). For example: "Since he cannot escape fatality, he will be his own fatality; since they have made life unlivable for him, he will live this impossibility of living as if he had created it expressly for himself, a particular ordeal reserved for him alone. He wills his destiny; he will try to love it" (pp. 499–500).

17. Genet, *Prisoner of Love*, p. 59.

18. See Sándor Ferenczi, *Thalassa*, tr. Henry Alden Bunker (London: Maresfield Library, 1989).

19. Georges Bataille, *Literature and Evil*, tr. Alastair Hamilton (London: Calder and Boyars, 1973), pp. 164, 161.

20. In "Remark on Rembrandt" (first published in *Tel Quel*, 1967), Genet asserts that there has never existed anything but a single man: each man is all other men, and a single man is divided infinitely, with all the other fragments appearing foreign to each of us. In the Rembrandt piece, this absorption of individuality in a universal homoness is seen as antagonistic to eroticism, whereas in *Funeral Rites* homo-ness is the dissemination of erotic energy.

21. Jean Genet, *Les Bonnes* (Paris: Marc Barbezat-Arbalète, 1947), p. 10. My translation.

22. Jean Genet, *The Maids and Deathwatch*, tr. Bernard Frechtman (New York: Grove/Weidenfeld, 1954), p. 45; Genet, *Les Bonnes*, p. 30. Subsequent page references to *The Maids* will be given in the text (translation and original in that order). Frechtman's translation is based on the 1954 version of the play, which is more sexually explicit and ends more triumphantly than the earliest 1947 text (now the standard French text). I will indicate any discrepancies between the two versions in the passages I quote.

23. In French: "Solange, tu me garderas en toi," and "Et surtout, quand tu seras condamnée, n'oublie pas que tu me portes en toi. Précieusement. Nous serons belles, libres et joyeuses" (pp. 110–111).

24. Thus Genet must even betray the Palestinian revolution in his "mirror-memoir" of the two years he spent living with Palestinian soldiers in Jordan and Lebanon, which he called *Un Captif amoureux* (in English, *Prisoner of Love*). He insists both that his account (contrary to what the Palestinians expected) "was never designed to tell the reader what the Palestinian revolution was really like" and that the revolution itself took place only so that the Palestinian mother and son in whose home Genet had spent a single night might "haunt" him for years afterward. Having broken with both Christianity and Islam, having reduced the Palestinian situation to a mere replication of his own obsession with the mutually protective relation between mother and son, he resignifies the Christian reference of that obsession (Christ and the Virgin) as the reoriginating, on the far side of a universal betrayal, of the coming-into-community of a universal human subject. Genet's love for Hamza and his mother, the "fixed mark" that has guided him, dates back to before Christ and is still "emitting radiations." "Had its

power," he wonders, "been building up over thousands of years?" (*Prisoner of Love,* pp. 331, 308, 177, 341).

25. Melanie Klein, "Early Analysis," in *Love, Guilt, and Reparation and Other Works, 1921–1945* (New York: Dell, 1975), p. 81.

26. Frechtman translates "Le livre est sincère et c'est une blague" (p. 194) as "This book is true and it's bunk" (p. 164).

Index